Dream Catcher 44

Stairwell Books //:

Dream Catcher 44

**Editor Emeritus
And Founder**
Paul Sutherland

Editor
Hannah Stone

Editorial Board
John Gilham (Retired Editor)
Amina Alyal (Retired Editor)
Tanya Parker Nightingale
Pauline Kirk
Rose Drew
Alan Gillott
Clint Wastling
Joe Williams
Caitlin Brown
Greg McGee

Art Advisor
Greg McGee

Production Managers
Alan Gillott and Rose Drew

Subscriptions to Dream Catcher Magazine

£15.00 UK (Two issues inc. p&p)
£22.00 Europe
£25.00 USA and Canada

Cheques should be made payable to **Dream Catcher** and sent to:

Dream Catcher Subscriptions
161 Lowther Street
York, YO31 7LZ
UK

+44 1904 733767

argillott@gmail.com

www.dreamcatchermagazine.co.uk
@literaryartsmag
www.stairwellbooks.co.uk
@stairwellbooks

Dream Catcher Magazine

Dream Catcher No. 44

©Angela Arnold, Belinda Cooke, Bill Fitzsimons, Chris Rice, Clare Wigzell, Clint Wastling, Daniel Richardson, Daniel Skyle, Diana Powell, Eileen Neil, Emmaline O'Dowd, Geoffrey Loe, George Jowett, Gerald Kells, Graham Buchan, Greg McGee, Gregory Heath, Hannah Stone, Heather Deckner, Helen Kay, Hélène Demetriades, Jennifer A Miller, Jenny Hockey, Joe Williams, John Lynch, John Scarsborough, John Whitehouse, Julie Venner, Kat Couch, Kelley J White, Ken Gambles, Maggie Davison, Mandy Haggith, Marion Ashton, Michael Church, Michael Penny, Moira Garland, Nick Allen, Noel King, Patrick Lodge, Pauline Kirk, Penny Blackburn, Peter Datyner, Philip Dunkerley, PJ Quinn, Ray Malone, Robert Lima, Roger Hare, Roy Duffield, Sarah L Dixon, Simon Currie, Stephanie Powell, Stewart Lowe, Stuart Handysides, Sue Spiers, Susan Wallace, Tanya Nightingale, Thomas Morgan, Tom Vaughan, Victoria Gatehouse, Will Kemp, Yvonne Hendrie, 2021

The moral rights of authors and artists have been asserted

ISSN: 1466-9455

Published by Stairwell Books //

ISBN: 978-1-913432-39-3

Contents – Authors

Featured Artist *Peter Davis*	1
Editorial	3
Futharc *Mandy Haggith*	Error! Bookmark not defined.
Piano Stool *Maggie Davison*	5
Saving the White Dress *Daniel Skyle*	6
Untold Stories Buried in the Mud and the Blood *Michael Church*	12
Hallstatt Abend *Robert Lima*	13
The Playground *Hélène Demetriades*	14
The Land of Green Ginger *Nick Allen*	15
Cut to the Hearth *Yvonne Hendrie*	18
The Rains *PJ Quinn*	19
The Purpose of Rain *Angela Arnold*	25
Stadium *Graham Buchan*	26
Pedal Power *Jennifer A Miller*	27
At the 11th Tee *Chris Rice*	28
The Patron Saint of Lost Things *Daniel Richardson*	29
Vision (that Was Planted in My Brain) *Philip Dunkerley*	30
Wind Farm *Kat Couch*	31
The Winds *Ray Malone*	32
The Tail End of Heaven *Moira Garland*	34
Not Dancing, 1959 *Jenny Hockey*	39
Glance *Tom Vaughan*	40
Strictly Come Dancing *John Whitehouse*	41
The Bells of Brescia *Clint Wastling*	46
Aftermath *John Scarsborough*	47
Pizza *Gregory Heath*	48
Waste *Stewart Lowe*	50
Thief *Stephanie Powell*	56
She Shoots the Crows *Penny Blackburn*	57
Parting of the Ways *Belinda Cooke*	58
Spring *Gerald Kells*	59
Resurrection, Easter 2020 *Susan Wallace*	60
Place *Clare Wigzell*	61
A Place I Know *Sarah L Dixon*	62

Street Sycamore *Emmaline O'Dowd*	63
Elder Mother *Victoria Gatehouse*	64
Hawthorns *Ken Gambles*	66
The Oak Said *Julie Venner*	67
The Wild *Geoffrey Loe*	68
The Poet, John Barlas, Arrives at Gartnavel Asylum *Helen Kay*	69
Pink Poppies *Marion Ashton*	70
Early Mornings *John Lynch*	71
Beware the Latinate *Simon Currie*	72
Sulphur *Tanya Nightingale*	73
Red Handed *Sue Spiers*	74
Dreaming of Befana *Roy Duffield*	75
Enfranchised *George Jowett*	76
My Muse *Michael Penny*	77
Another Bone *Bill Fitzsimons*	78
Tryst *Noel King*	79
I Want That Espresso Machine *Thomas Morgan*	81
In the Stranger's Hand *Heather Deckner*	84
Waiting Rooms *Peter Datyner*	85
Angelic Spaces and Infinite Geometries *Roger Hare*	86
I'm Fine; Thanks for Asking *Stuart Handysides*	87
Girl Before the Mirror i, ii and iii *Diana Powell*	88
Exposure *Will Kemp*	93
After the Pandemic *Eileen Neil*	96
Ashes to Go *Kelley J White*	97
Reviews	98
Cloud Cuckoo Café by **Linda Marshall** *Joe Williams*	99
Cures by **Jo Brandon** *Hannah Stone*	100
When I Think of My Body as a Horse by **Wendy Pratt** *Clint Wastling*	101
between two rivers by **Nick Allen and Myles Linley** *Pauline Kirk*	102
These Mothers of Gods by **Rachel Bower** *Hannah Stone*	102
The Stranger in my Head by **Simon Passmore** *Nick Allen*	103
New Chapbooks from The Poetry Business *Patrick Lodge*	104
Index of Authors	108

Featured Artist
Artist Statement: Peter Davis

Solitude not only heals, it galvanises and kindles. And in a time when hurrying into a day filled with coffee and deadlines is the norm, a quiet cup of tea on the couch can be a countercultural act.

Solitude can be creativity's ground zero, where the first seeds are sown, and a harvest reaped at leisure. Wordsworth was onto something when he rhapsodised "I wandered lonely as a cloud" – in a few lines of extreme, lyrical simplicity he nails that moment when we witness in the wilderness of wandering something worth writing about. He sees "the host of golden daffodils;" he recentres; and, following his own maxim of "emotion recollected in tranquility", later mints some of the most bullet proof poetry of the last 250 years.

Solitude too is the subject matter of Peter Davis's collection of paintings, 'Zeitgeist', but these young people are not in touch with their poetic muse, rather they are totally distracted by digital devices. Depending on your age or outlook, these could work as cautionary images, moments of envy (Snapchat! Fortnite!), moments of simple communication, or a bit of meta-imagery. It is the latter that equips 'Zeitgeist' with a crucial poetic thrust.

Via Davis' forensic observation and painterly mark making, a doubleness emerges. It is Painting and its analogue physicality that captures thralldom to all things digital. It is Davis' hand held skills, hewn from countless hours in the studio, that fixes the flickering ephemerality of pressing, swiping, saving, deleting. Unlike Wordsworth, Davis wields all of his prowess to immortalise not the world of universal aesthetics (flowers, trees, skies) but this new world of digital experience, where thrills, boredom, and communication intersect. This is Virtual Reality depicted in realistic painting.

It's in the act of painting that something is reclaimed in these subjects. Our first impression of their drone-like focus on devices is expertly offset by Davis' consummate brush strokes. The very heft of his palette and the marks he makes engenders in his subjects a quickening, bringing them to pulsing life, thus softening our initial reaction. This is the genius of Davis' output. Perhaps there is after all poetry to be found in the simple joy of reaching for what is to many a direct line to expressing that 'something worth writing about', and for a generation from whom so much has been stolen, time spent on the Cloud is as healing as time wandering lonely as one.

Greg McGee, June 2021

PAGES OF ARTWORK

Kindlelight	16
The Red Door – Old Rowntree's Factory	33
Wetin Dey – Solomon Onaolapo	49
101 Harper Street	65
Me (mise en abyme)	*80*
Late Night Screening	Cover

EDITORIAL

Dream Catcher 44 seems to have been afflicted with an outbreak of nostalgia; could it be reflecting a world wearied by the tenacity of the pandemic, which lingers like a bad odour round the boarded-up shops and travel agencies of our towns? Many of the poems and stories that made the cut hark back to imaginary or remembered ages (golden as well as not so shiny), or feature elements of the fantastic and macabre – preferred modes of living, waiting like untried on clothes in the wardrobe, their purchase labels swinging in the draught of the opened door. Of course, there's the usual smattering of realism, too, with hearts (broken and intact), endings, the lessons of the natural world, high jinks and dancing, and the hope of resurrection (or at least change of a sort). Perhaps we were channelling Richard Strauss' tone poem, *Death and Transfiguration*, with reminiscences of childhood shoving against the challenges of adulthood, and finally a coming to terms with some sort of maturity and afterlife.

Once again we have attracted writers and readers from all over the globe. Spread the word, friends. The current submission window is open until the end of February when my stalwart team of readers will make final selections of work for DC 45. As before, send your paper submissions (if at all possible) to the editor at 109 Wensley Drive, Leeds LS7 2LU, and all enquiries about subscriptions, changes of address, beefs about the government, and bright ideas for saving the planet, etc. to the good folk at Stairwell in York. Happy reading and writing.

Hannah Stone

FUTHARC

a fang hangs in a glass case
an amulet engraved with runic ABC
a dentine key
to unlock a Viking
abracadabra

out in front, a pianist
conjures *allegro maestoso, andante, presto*
years of secret practice
concealed by ivory
and cool notation

the tooth evokes
the medicine woman who wore it
strung on a leather thong
in rituals to spring cubs out of darkness
and bite back life, letter by letter

behind the piano
the past seethes
air crackles like static in fur –
the presence of a shaman
a shadow of a bear

Mandy Haggith

*futharc, these first symbols of the runic alphabet are engraved on a bear's tooth in the National Museum of Scotland, where occasional music recitals are held.

Piano Stool

On her mother's piano stool
is a girl with too much time,
bouncing on its frayed brocade,
scuffing its Queen Anne legs.

She piles dolls on cushions,
porcelain fingers on cold keys;
teddies with glassy eyes stare
at the stand, the dots and squiggles.

She heaps the chants of classmates
onto the silent piano players,
the cut of skipping rope
against bare flesh in the big yard.

And then, on top, she puts
Mrs Crisp's sharp tongue,
hovering above her head, spitting
threats about lost schoolbooks.

Inside the stool, squashed between
years of sheet music, is Eileen Joyce:
wrists poised, chestnut curls pinned up,
a gown of Beethoven blue sliding

from her tiny frame. Sometimes,
the girl gazes at the picture, inspired
to practise her scales and arpeggios.
She'll not take Eileen out today.

Maggie Davison

SAVING THE WHITE DRESS
A short story from the Books of Excalibur

Archive Section F5/1243 [OPERATION SOPHIE]: interview from tape with Amélie Marguerite Dieudonné de Valois, member of the Healing Group. Interview done in 1953. Stored M8F5/1243 Church House Station, Charing Cross, London. REF: HEAL 2012, OPERATION SOPHIE, OPERATION GOLGATA, root: Amélie De Valois 1-42.

Okay. Well, the arch-duke would die anyway, we knew that from the go. My goal was to save her, and her white dress, from an eternity of black-and-white photographs. We knew that if we could prevent the blood from spreading over her dress, World War I would be a lot milder. We could save millions. Millions.

And that task fell to me.

The sun was shining really strong and clear that day. I will try to keep this to the point, but I think it might be helpful for those who listen to this later to get some detail of how things looked, what we saw with our own eyes. Maybe, just maybe, the chance of someone repeating our mistake is smaller, then.

Our mistake must never be repeated.

So, the sun fell over Sarajevo, making the Miljacka shine that day. The Miljacka is the river that cuts the city in two like a wedding band. The sun was shining in the eyes of the crowds along the route, and the flags all the children held looked like they were dancing even though there was no wind.

The morning of the 28th was a beautiful, beautiful June morning.

The 28th of June, 1914.

The arch-duke and crown prince of the Austro-Hungarian empire, Franz Ferdinand, was coming to visit Sarajevo. Serbian emotions had run high for several years already, you see, after the Austro-Hungarian annexation of Bosnia-Hercegovina, and some of the cast members of that show were running wild on the city streets.

Seven assassins, each of whom wanted to be midwife to a new, proud Great Serbia. Six assassins and one boss, a piece of shit called Danilo Ilic whom we had papers on from local sources in their intelligence services.

Illic was in the Black Hand, a kind of secret death squad. Illic came to a bad end later, thank the gods, but that is a whole different story. I will try to keep us on this one.

Alors. One of the seven was called Gavrilo Princip. He was barely twenty years old and obsessed, completely obsessed, you see, about creating a new great Slavic empire.

We didn't know his name, or his appearance.

We only knew that a group was planning the assassination that day. Somewhere, somehow, at an unspecified time. In Sarajevo.

Not much about our missions change over the centuries, does it?

So there I was, young and dumb and very wet behind the ears, running around Sarajevo with my long hair flying in the wind. I was moving that fast, with all my senses on wide alert as we tried to find the nodal point.

Our seers at the time had judged it to be Linden VI, a code so high I don´t think it has been used since, not even during the war that came after. Not even during Golgotha, and we saw enough problems then, too.

We knew it was so strong it could affect the whole "great war" they scryed. "The war that will end all other wars". As if they ever stop: stupidity is eternal. However, this nodal point could prevent so much death, so much destruction, so much awful suffering, that we had *eight* full teams out there. 25-30 members, can you imagine? Including some Lone Wolves, plus several in astral shape on overwatch. It was almost the entire European section of the Healing Group in the early 20th century, all of us out looking for this nodal point that might stop World War I ...

Oh, we had people in Budapest, Vienna, the Italian countryside; a team ended up in Tuzla, which later turned out to be because Princip was born in a small village nearby. They had the most boring day of their life, they told me later.

I had been allotted to Sarajevo, with Jochem there as Senior. I was so young. So new. Only ten years into Excalibur. Five years apprentice, five years full member. A mere child, I was, compared with most of the other ones who had decades of missions behind them.

Alors. The arch-duke and his wife Sofia were visiting Sarajevo.

They were there to meet the mayor, be seen, wave, wear shiny epaulettes, huge mustaches, a stunning white dress, and to represent the power of empire in general.

And I ran.

I ran in the town. We knew that food was involved in some way, the seers had said that. But we had no idea how. Or why. Just "the danger probably involves food."

The event nodal point was possible to affect through a café, a restaurant, or something like that. To affect nodal points is to affect the seed of what will be. It's part of what we do in the Healing Group, of course, but it's not everyone who understands how important this is, I can tell you. It looks like a boring job. Sometimes it can be to put a newspaper on a bench by a bus stop. Or to stand on an abandoned railway platform and give the wrong direction to someone getting off a train. Or the right one.

It all depends, *non*?

We can be a tiny piece of well-placed grit in the machinery of destiny. Correctly placed, we make certain huge events never happen, and through that, save one, or thousands or hundreds of thousands of lives. And sometimes we make sure something happens that has to happen and almost wouldn't. Alexandria was one of those. The books were saved and hidden so that Christianity never destroyed them. You would be amazed at how much oil it takes to get a good fire going in a stone building, I hear *[Laughter]*.

So, to look for nodal points, and to heal. But everyone knows about the healing, you see; few understand that the real focus is the nodal points. If we can heal the world through them, we save so much, both time and lives and suffering.

We had two teams in Vienna when Hitler was there; young, dirt poor and still full of bright artist dreams... And we never found him. He lived in a dingy bed-and-breakfast where the Jewish owner lent his second-best coat to the skinny Austrian yokel so he wouldn't freeze to death.

The bitter irony of it, eh?

But on this day that gave birth to everything, I wandered along the Miljacka when I heard the mumbling rise. They came driving straight out of the sun, you see. You had to squint a lot to see the cortege. Only three cars, but a car was a very big deal back then. The crowd was going wild around me.

That's when I saw the group.

I could feel them, even at a distance. They were... Not standing next to each other, but in about a fifty meter radius, probably to cover as many roads as possible.

I felt it. I felt them. I can't describe how desperate I became and how small I felt.

We knew that the arch-duke couldn't be saved, you see. He was sentenced to death no matter what we did. But if we could reach the nodal point, Sophie, his wife, could be saved, and that was some kind of shift point, if we could counter her death. A genuine dragon hole, like the Chinese change masters call it. If we could do this, it would make the war, the absolute horror of this enormous awful war, not become as horrible as, well, as it turned out to be.

So much death, so much grief. I was there during the war, doing the work of the Healing Group on the Western Front. But that's a much longer story than this one, and you'll have to interview me again for that. I haven't got time to stay that long today. Meeting old friends at the Ritz later, friends from the war that came after the War to End All Wars. *[short laugh on the tape]*

So, the conspirators.

I see how one man suddenly ran away. One of them gave up; I only found out afterwards that Jochem managed to use his powers to change the man's mind. Because of the stress, he made it so strong that the man travelled all the way back home to his small mountain village before stopping.

And just when I was getting a glimmer of hope – what if we had *stopped* it? – I see the hand grenade fly through the air over everybody's heads. I see the grenade, believe it or not, I actually see the sun shine on it. And I felt ... How all of me just froze. Despite all my training, I just froze. I had failed. That's what I thought.

But it missed. We know that now. It bounced on the arch-duke's car enough to blow up under the car behind them instead, where it exploded and threw steel fragmentation through the crowd, levelling it to the ground.

I can still hear the screams.

And everything becomes chaos, you see. Everybody runs all over the place like headless chickens. I used this as camouflage to get out of there, once I saw the royal car screech off. Praise be gilt epaulettes sometimes!

So I walked from there straight into the old alleyways. Sarajevo in 1914 was a dump, believe you me.

My head was a complete mess and I could still feel the pain from all those lying with shrapnel wounds down by the Miljacka, so I bounced like a pinball from café to café, entered restaurants, sniffed around, wandered out. Even went into the pubs, even though the men there stared at me in shock since I was a woman. But no-one, no-one I could feel who had the flavour of the conspirators.

But something...

Something kept telling me that time was running out, you see. It felt like we were losing the node. It shone in my mind like a star, and still it felt like it was slipping out of my hands.

So I walked quickly down yet another nameless alley, wondering what the hell Jochem was doing. And a small part of me prayed intensely that the famous Jochem has simply solved everything, and when I turn up, I can just collapse in a pile in a corner and ignore saving the world for six months.

So. By now, it was about 10.30 local time.

The arch-duke and Sophie were at the hospital, we found out later. They wanted to visit the onlookers who were hurt by the grenade.

In my daze I walk past a delicatessen – Schiller's, I still remember the name after all this time – and I turned back. It had to do with food, after all. You never knew.

When I came in, little old ladies stood there whispering while the staff behind the counter looked very worried. I asked what had happened, in my then very strong French accent, and they told me they just had a young man in there – a young man with a gun stuffed down his shirt! He had bought a pastrami sandwich, and then left, and he had a gun!

What did he look like. WHAT DID HE LOOK LIKE? WHAT DID HE LOOK LIKE?!

Then I ran.

I could feel the direction to go. I don't think I have ever run as fast in my life as I did then. Never.

I wish I could have run faster.

I am just in time to see Operation Sophie fail in front of me. Jochem is a hundred meters further down the river, I found out later. He was there when they caught one of the co-conspirators who tried to drown himself in two decimeter of Miljacka water.

But I was only ten meters away from the car.

I saw World War I begin.

Princíp is small, thin, and uncertain, an overgrown teenager. A child, really, weak face, thin little mustache. Malnourished. But he had power enough to lift the gun. Hate gives so much power. So terribly much power.

The arch-duke's car had turned around, and was heading back over the bridge. Later, we found out it had been a mistake, the driver had misunderstood and taken a wrong turn ... And turned around straight back at Princíp.

I see him run straight up to the car, just before it drives over the bridge. He shoots, I see his intent to almost throw himself into the car like a terrier, the gun out-stretched in a tense arm. The arch-duke looks surprised, Sophia terrified, and their bodyguard saw nothing, he was looking in the other direction, out over the river.

The first shot hits her. I see her fall.

I stand there, 29 years old, and see our whole mission vanish before my eyes.

The whole of my life, I´ve fought with this moment.

[Silence on the tape, 49 seconds.]

Fought with ... That everything wasn´t my fault ... That I wasn´t guilty of World War I ... I know, I know. I know everything we teach and all the training we get and all that. I have been a member of Excalibur twice as long as you have been alive, young man. But still. If you had been there, you would also have fought with it for the rest of your life, trust me. But we all have our cross to bear. Everybody gets their very own karma to work with.

Well. He shot them, of course. Sophie, Sophie who I should have saved, falls with a flower of blood on her belly. The bullet kills two: it murders her unborn child too.

Flowers of blood on the white dress. And the whole war afterwards comes to be coded into the poppy flowers on Flanders Fields. That is a black irony, isn´t it?

The second shot hit the arch-duke. He dies within a minute. Afterwards, we find out that his last words to her was that she should live for their child. Sophie dies on her way to hospital.

Alors. That is probably the whole story. This is the way it was for me, and I was there. I became a witness to it, and I became one of those guilty that it happened. After Operation Sophie, I worked through the entire war in different places to try to heal the situation and make it milder as best we could. We lost 12 members from the Healing Group during World War I, one of the worst strikes against us since the 1300´s and the Black Death.

Jochem worked just like me, and then continued with World War II too, until a sniper killed him. Killed him lying in the soot-covered grass on Sword Beach on D-Day.

Princíp? They put him in jail, of course.

Pure miracle the crowd didn´t tear him limb from limb there and then. But he was put in prison and sentenced to twenty years. He died in 1918, the same year the war ended.

The irony of fate, *non?*

But I remember that morning still. A sunny morning in June, it was, the 28th of June 1914, when I watched World War I begin.

And I remember how I was young and ran through Sarajevo with my hair flying behind me, and I remember the pastrami sandwich and the poppy.

We should have succeeded. But we didn't.

Interviewer´s notation: Recording ends there. Amélie de Valois worked actively up until her death in 1958. She chose to move on rather than stay and work for Excalibur in the Long Service. It is believed that the failure to stop the murder of Sophie was a factor in her decision. Frederic D'Arrignac/FDA 1953/1962.

Daniel Skyle

Untold Stories Buried in the Mud and the Blood

They walked the beach that night
knowing they would embark at dawn
on foreign shores a flash of light
the piper's tune sounded forlorn.

Knowing they would embark at dawn
to fight the politicians' fight
the piper's tune sounded forlorn
young men with futures bright.

To fight the politicians' fight
waging war to protect the Crown
young men with futures bright
futures gone their lives laid down.

Waging war to protect the Crown,
dead soldiers with faces white
futures gone their lives laid down
Staring up with unblinking sight

Dead soldiers with faces white
on foreign shores a flash of light
staring up with unblinking light
they walked the beach that night.

Michael Church

Hallstatt Abend

From the private garden by Hallstatter See,
the open sky is swept with lilting pigments–
uncommon hues against the blue and white–
coming ever closer in their aerial sweeps,
descending towards the granite mountains
to be nearly lost within the lower backdrop
of the firs that reach majestically to heights.

Houses, multi-hued, perched jauntily, proclaim
themselves against the hills that top the lake.

The tall dark steeple of the lakeside church
pierces to the sky, the granite tor above.

*

The parasails that spiral to the waterside
glide apace like summer light along the crags.

Orange train across the lake. A log-brown fuhr
lazes passengers across the grey-green See.

Glass-like, water mirrors mountain colors
till a trout jumps up and breaks the glaze,
leaving circles in the Hallstatt eve.

Robert Lima

The Playground

The year we left the mountains

a new playground was set
      among young trees

    on the other side
of the road from the gushing stream;

a red slide, shiny roundabout, set of swings.

We scaled the birches for a dare
  curious
     where our pee would fall;

  mine spilt
      down the silver trunk
  like a christening.

I didn't recognise it
   as my future grief,

  a torrent of burning water
for the land I would lose.

Hélène Demetriades

The Land of Green Ginger

sliding into Paragon station 35 years later   there is no sign of the pub that bore the name   from where double-deckers wheezed onto the streets from bent old railings where expectation leant with its hot greasy chips and cold easterly thighs   the last ride swaying up Bev Road   West down Spring Bank   to Bransholme or trips to Hornsea   Withernsea   go now before they fall into the sea   it is a *shopping experience* with Krispy Kreme Donuts and other illiterate spending opportunities I-brow threading & nail barz   not an ounce of romance in its shiny interior polished by an army of zero-hour workers
                                                                              the first time I came here under my own steam   Larkin was alive   still ploughing his misogyny for metaphors   now be-statued in front of Starbucks he looks like a vital man in motion   back then I shared a carriage with another visiting would-be student   a flame-haired daughter of Rochdale called Sarah whose vowels dipped like the Trough of Bowland   we were seventeen and out in the adult world on probation   I spent the journey wondering if we would have sex but lacking the courage to ask   now stepping out of the station I see scattered groups of Witnesses asking *will suffering end*   and I tell them   they are in the right place to find out

Nick Allen

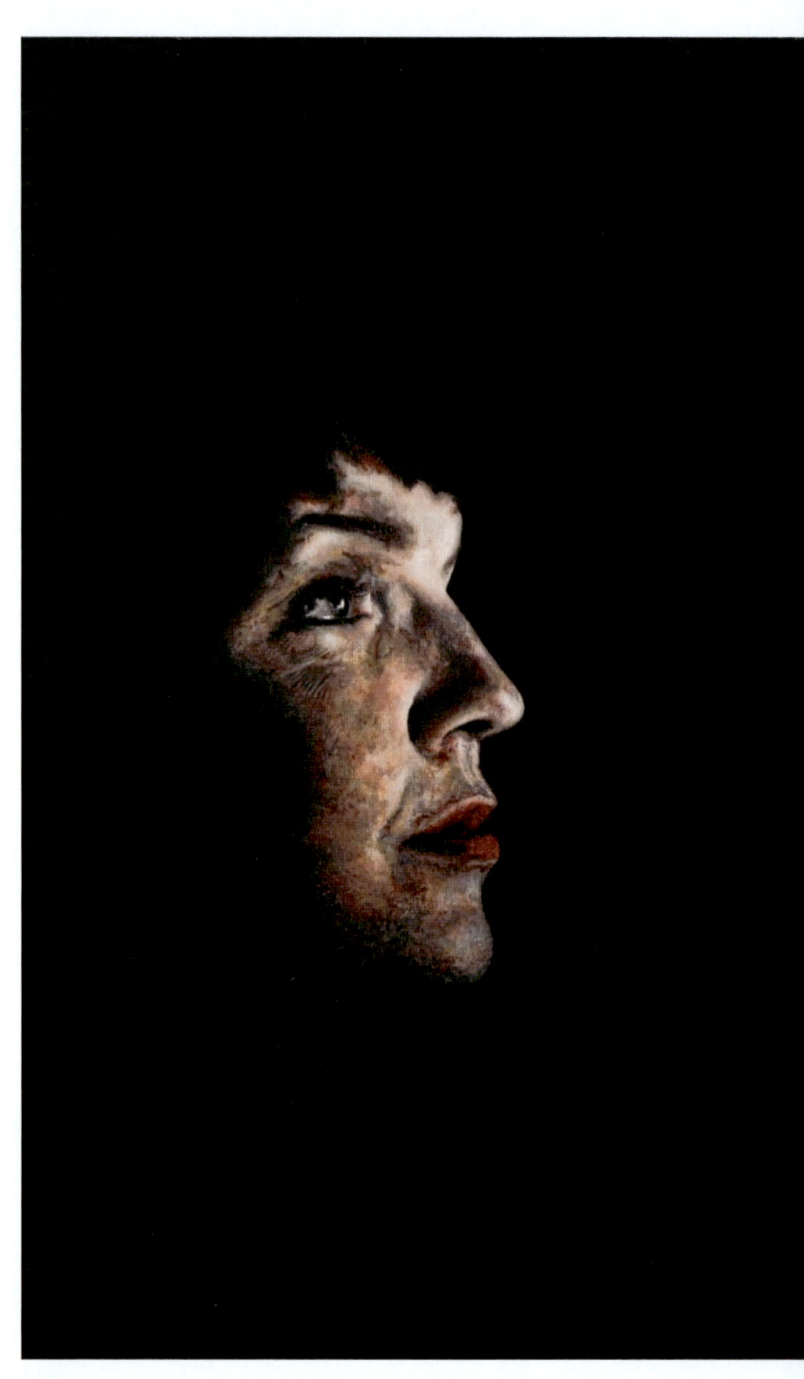

Kindlelight

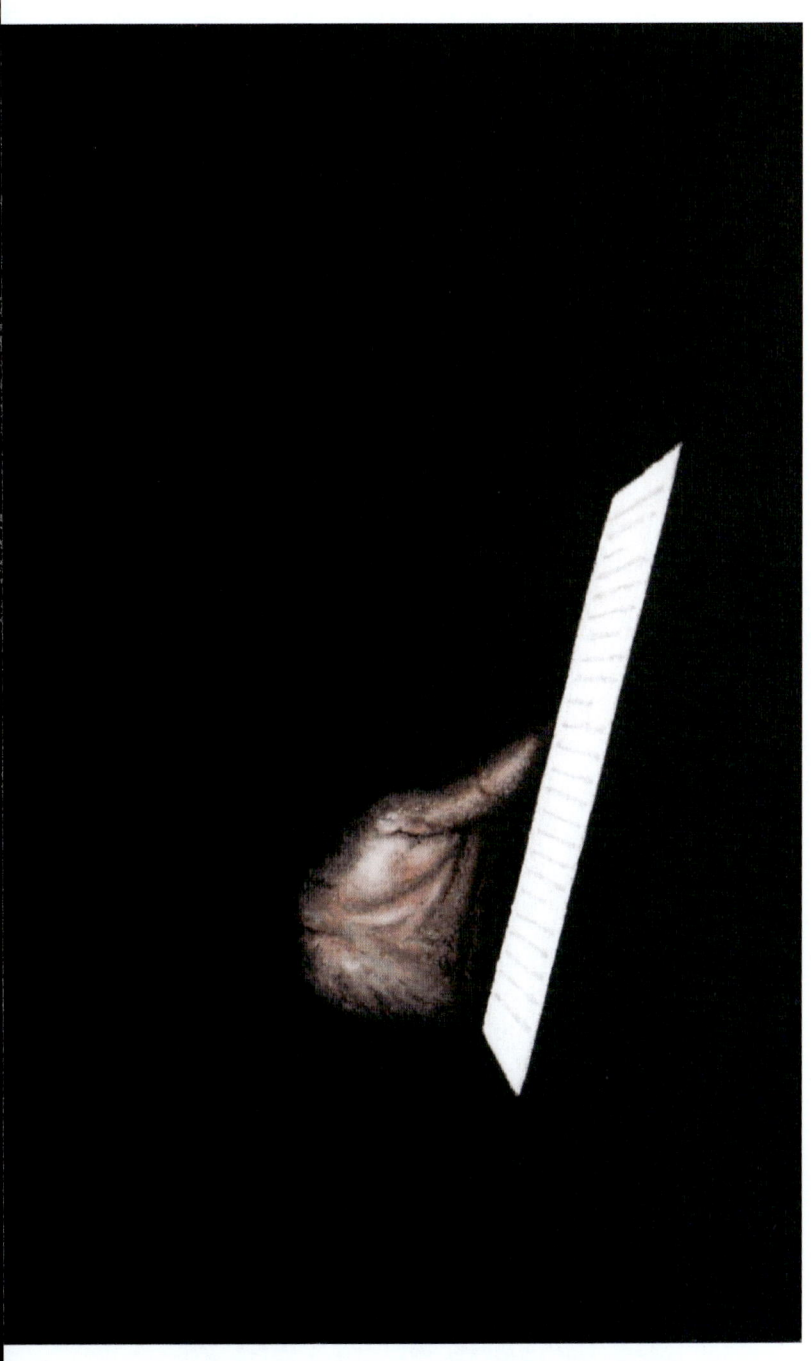

Cut to the Hearth

Demolition dissected the old tenement,
gable end exposed to a grey Glasgow day.
Black veins ran from ghost fireplaces
to a forest of blasted chimneys on the roof.
Lums, we call them here, their soot
sliced through and tracing
pathways for all to see;
dust from decades of fires
once roaring in those ghostly grates,
blackened like congealed blood.
And the hearths that blazed on Hogmanays,
saw lumps of coal added then for luck –
"Lang may yer lum reek!"
toasted bread on forks for breakfasts,
dried bairns' nappies, and long johns;
where lassies held their heads as close
as they dared to dry their hair before the dancin';
hearths that witnessed home births, and deaths –
now gape cold and empty, their memories
long wafted away, fallen and trampled
in sooty city downpours.

Yvonne Hendrie

Reg was washing his new car; again. It was the second time this week. Not that the car was dirty, Ian thought. After all, it was less than a month old and had hardly been used. Still, if Ian had a brand-new red sports car, he'd probably be out cleaning it every day too. He glanced at his ancient Volvo in the drive and shrugged. Turning, he saw his daughter doing her school homework at the kitchen table and remembered why he couldn't afford a new sports car. He would rather pay for her schooling.

"Hey, Dad," Gabrielle called, "come and look at this."

Ian left the window and crossed to his daughter. He was immensely proud of Gabrielle. Like her sadly deceased mother, she was thin and elegant with jet black hair. At fourteen she was just starting to turn from girl to young woman. Ian knew it wouldn't be long before she started taking an interest in boys. The boys had been taking an interest in her for a couple of years. Fortunately, she'd also inherited her father's love of books and, so far, hadn't noticed.

"What am I meant to be looking at?" he asked.

"This bit on ancient fairy tales and myths. We've been asked to find old stories that can still be relevant today, for a project. I've just been reading about the legend of St. Swithin. Did you know that if it rains on St. Swithin's Day, it will rain for forty days and forty nights?"

"So I've heard. When is St. Swithin's Day?"

"Today."

Ian put his hand on his daughter's head. "Let's hope it doesn't rain," he teased. "Fortunately, we're forecast fine weather for the next three days. I'm afraid you're out of luck."

***

Dominic was poking the ground with a stick. "What are you doing?" his mother asked.

"Play ants," he replied.

They were sitting in the shelter of the cricket pavilion. Julia leaned over to see what Dominic was looking at. She immediately recoiled. She hadn't expected to see so many ants.

"Darling, I don't think you should poke the ants with a stick," she said and removed the stick from her son's hand. "You don't want to make them angry. Look! Some of them have wings, so they could fly at you if you poke them too hard."

Dominic looked upset at the loss of his stick. Julia quickly replaced it with a small slice of pork pie. Her son brightened and started munching.

Julia looked back at the ants. They were marching purposefully in a line across the terrace, towards the trees behind the pavilion. As she looked closer, she could see that some of them were carrying small white balls on their backs. She wondered if those were ant eggs and, if so, why the whole colony of ants was moving towards the trees.

She read the ledger again and sighed. It didn't matter how many times she checked; the numbers stayed the same. Putting the ledger back in her bag she looked around. The old club hut wasn't bad, but it could definitely do with a lick of paint and some new furniture. There was no hope of either, given the club's finances. She wasn't sure why she'd let herself be persuaded (or was it bullied?) into being the club's Treasurer.

Sighing, Julia glanced at the trees. All was quiet. She wondered why she couldn't hear the usual babble of birds. The sky was darkening, clouds mounding like grey candyfloss. After a month of dry sunny weather there was a chill in the air. It was quite a shock; it didn't feel like July at all. "Come along darling," she said to Dominic. "We'd better head home. Race you to the corner." Pretending to run, she hurried along the path towards the road, little Dominic trotting alongside her.

As they rounded the corner of the cricket field, a sudden wind blew. Startled, a squadron of angry crows rose into the sky, screeching. Julia watched as they circled over her. For some reason, she shuddered. "It looks like rain," she said over brightly, "and I haven't brought an umbrella. What a silly Mummy!"

Picking her son up, she quickened her pace.

***

Reg was gently stroking his new pride and joy. Who cared if the wife had wanted to go on a cruise? It was his pension lump sum, not hers, after all. And he'd always, always wanted a new sports car. A convertible of course, but not a soft top. He didn't trust them; thought they'd probably leak in the rain. So, he'd treated himself to a model which converted at the flick of a switch. He still loved watching the top go in and out of its little hidey-hole at the back.

Now all he needed was some nice weather to go zooming around in. He couldn't wait to see the neighbours' faces; they'd be so jealous. He'd seen Ian staring from his front window on the other side of the road. Well, let him ogle, Reg smiled to himself.

He glanced at the sky. A large cloud was forming. It looked like a hammer head: that often meant thunder, he recalled. He considered putting the new love of his life into the garage, but the lawn mower was still in bits on the floor. He'd have to get round to mending that first, and he'd far rather polish the car. Besides, rain wasn't forecast until Tuesday. The weatherman on TV had joked about missing St Swithin's Day.

***

"It looks like we may be safe after all," Ian remarked after lunch.
"What do you mean, Dad?" Gabrielle looked up, surprised.

"The sky's a little lighter. We'll be spared your forty days and nights of rain."

"Good, except that if it doesn't rain, I won't be able to prove whether the myth is true," Gabrielle replied, smiling. "I was hoping it would rain a bit, but then be sunny and warm for the rest of the summer, just to show the whole St Swithin thing is rubbish."

"I'm with you in wanting a nice summer," Ian agreed. "By the way, have you seen the ant powder? There's a lot of ants coming into the lounge from behind the skirting board."

"I think it's in the shed." Gabrielle looked up. "You'll also need some in the kitchen and the hallway. I saw some ants there earlier. They seemed to be intent on going up the walls. I have no idea why."

"Maybe they know better than the forecasters," Ian suggested, "and they're going for higher ground. Maybe you'll be able to test St. Swithin after all."

He was smiling as he went out to the shed.

***

"You know, I think St Swithin may have had a point," Gabrielle exclaimed. She was standing at the kitchen window later that afternoon, watching the sky. Rather than going away as her father had hoped, the clouds had thickened. The room was going dark, though it was only four o'clock. "If it does rain it'll be heavy." She glanced over her shoulder at her father.

"I hope we don't get forty days and nights of it, or there'll be floods," Ian replied, only half joking.

"It's a good job we're not on the other side of the road. They always get loads of water in their drives when it rains heavily." He tried not to sound anxious. "Do you remember where I put that ant powder by the way?"

"What?" Gabrielle was surprised, not with her father losing the powder (that was par for the course) but that he needed it again. She left her vigil at the kitchen window and followed him into the hall. Then she stopped in astonishment. Each corner was black. It was too dark to see why, so she put the light on. At once a flurry of ants scurried back under the skirting boards. Others headed for the gap in the floorboards near the stairs.

"We don't have that much powder," Gabrielle said in alarm. "I've never seen so many ants."

Recalling her biology classes, she tried to remember if there was anything else they could use. Perhaps if they looked at the ingredients on the box, they might be able to make something themselves. "Why have they come in?" she asked.

"I've no idea, but they seem to be going upwards," her father replied. "Maybe they're expecting a storm and are trying to stay dry."

"Shall we leave them to it, or kill them?" Gabrielle asked. "It seems unfair to wipe them out, but I don't want ants in my bed." She grimaced at the thought. "But if they keep moving upwards, they'll end up in the attic, which is probably ok. I don't see they can do any damage there. Can we just leave them?"

"We may not have much choice," her father decided. "We don't have enough powder to keep them at bay forever. I don't think these are stinging ants, although I don't like the look of the ones with wings. If they just keep to the corners, we can step round them. It's not ideal, but I don't know what else to suggest. We could try putting sticky tape around things we don't want them on."

"I think you'd have to keep replacing the sticky tape," Gabrielle warned. "When the tape's full of dead ants, the others can just climb over them."

"What a horrible thought!" Ian replied, just as the telephone rang.

Gabrielle answered. "It's Julia from next door, Dad," she whispered. "She's really worried because they have ants everywhere and her little boy keeps playing with them. She doesn't know what to do. What shall I say?"

"Tell her she's welcome here, but we're in the same position. Though thankfully you're too old to play with ants these days."

Gabrielle snorted and turned back to the telephone.

"That's decided then," she announced as she put the phone down. "Julia and Dominic are coming round. She's going to bring any ant powder she can find. I'll make up the spare bed in the guest room for her, and she can put Dominic on the little sofa beside her."

His daughter's quiet efficiency impressed Ian. He wondered whether she was trying to match-make. Certainly, Julia was attractive, although about 10 years younger than him. More importantly she was divorced and, according to Gabrielle, this made her "available" for a lonely widower. Smiling, he stepped over a column of ants and ruffled his daughter's hair.

An hour later, Dominic was playing happily in the middle of the lounge. Gabrielle had found a box of toys from the recesses of her cupboard, annoying a hundred or so ants in the process. Julia had been in such a state that she'd arrived with nothing other than her son in her arms and two puffers of ant powder.

"I hate ants," Julia sighed. "Especially the ones with wings! They're absolutely everywhere in my house."

"As you can see," Ian replied, "we've got quite a few of our own. It's ok though," he added, seeing her concern, "they keep to the corners of the rooms, mainly on the skirting boards. We're leaving them alone and they're returning the compliment."

Gabrielle appeared, carrying a large sports bag filled with whatever she'd thought Julia and Dominic would need. She glanced quizzically at her father.

"I bet she's trying to work out how well I'm getting on with Julia," Ian thought.

**

Reg was incandescent with rage. He'd spent an hour reassembling the lawn mower so he could put his pride and joy into the garage. But when he'd got into the car, the engine wouldn't start. He couldn't believe it. A brand-new sports car which goes from 0-60 in less than five seconds, and there it was, sitting on his drive unable to go anywhere. So, he'd run back into the house to get his wife to help push the car into the garage. Only she'd refused. She'd also suggested it might just need a good wash. It must be at least a couple of hours since he last did it. He was not impressed with her attitude.

Contemplating his next move Reg stood at the front door. He'd seen a number of people come and go at Ian's over the road. Maybe they'd help him push his car into the garage? He decided it was worth trying, and ran across the road, not stopping to tell his wife.

He arrived panting on Ian's doorstep. It was Gabrielle who opened the porch door. She looked surprised but let him into the hallway. "Hey Dad," she called out, "it's Mr Dutton from over the road."

"Come on in," she said to Reg,

Ian appeared in the hallway with Julia behind him. "We're having an impromptu house-party," he said drily. "You're welcome to join us."

Reg didn't stop to ask why Ian had his pretty neighbour at his house; he figured that she and Ian were healthy and strong enough to help push his car. He was about to ask for their assistance when he heard Gabrielle gasp. She'd closed the porch, but the front door was open. Her hand still on the doorknob, she was looking towards Reg's house. "That's strange," she said.

"What is, honey?" her father asked.

"I thought Mr Dutton's new car was red, but it's got black patches on it now."

Reg turned with astonishment. It was true. His car was black on the bonnet and doors, rather than the beautiful fire red that he'd paid for. There was no way anyone could have swapped the car when he wasn't looking, was there? He could feel anger brewing up inside him. Maybe his wife was playing a trick on him? Or someone had splashed paint on it?

"Hang on," Ian said. He reached for a pair of binoculars from the top drawer of the hall cupboard. He was focussing on the car when Reg pulled the binoculars out of his hand. Surprised, Ian protested but Reg didn't reply.

It was hard to see through the porch glass, but it looked to Reg as if his car was quivering. Bewildered, he handed the binoculars back to Ian. "Take a look," he said. Ian took them with a wry smile: he'd been trying to look when Reg snatched the binoculars from him. His smile faded. "That's odd," he said. "Your car definitely has black patches on it."

"I can see that," Reg snapped back. "What I can't see is why."

Ian shrugged and passed the binoculars to his daughter. She had better eyesight than he did. Gabrielle re-focussed the lenses and stared intently across the road.

"Oh …" she said softly and put her hand to her mouth. Ian turned to her in concern. "The car's covered in ants, Dad," she whispered. "That's why it's got black patches. They seem to be trying to climb onto the hood and slipping. Maybe they do know something we don't. I think we should move everything valuable upstairs …" She realised Reg had heard.

"I'm sure everything will be ok, Mr Dutton," she added quickly.

Reg pushed past them both. It was alright for her to say everything would be ok; she hadn't just spent over a hundred grand on a new car. He wasn't going to have it covered in ants. Goodness only knew what they'd do to it. They were probably already in the engine, which was why it wouldn't start. He ran over the road towards his house, oblivious to everything but the car on his drive. He was scarcely aware of the squeal of brakes as a van swerved to avoid him. He dimly heard Gabrielle scream, but he was too intent on the black dots swarming over the bonnet to care. Grabbing a broom from the garage he started trying to brush them off. "Go away!" he shouted. "Get off!"

His wife appeared at a window. "We've got ants all over the house!" she shouted. "They're everywhere, even on the stairs. Leave that stupid car and do something!"

But Reg wasn't listening. He was staring at the thousands of ants crawling inside his new car.

Suddenly fat spots of water splashed onto his head.

It was beginning to rain…

PJ Quinn

The Purpose of Rain

You see the fat of the river punctured, its tight skin
needled. You watch drops, drops
piling on drops, throwing wild water patterns
into yet more water, no sense
at all, this teeming down, this hammering wet
courting an even wetter –
an insult to the sensible eye, this grand waste.
Target missed, surely.

Good rain on parched ground; bad
rain ... playing games?

And still dollops sing, and dollops' picture dances, crooks
an enticing finger: this is where the action is,
among all these falling children
plummeting
on to their great riverskin trampoline –
such a bounce to them
(while you feign work too close to your window)
before they sink, slow, calm, dive
home, the thing you've never yet named
for yourself. Properly. And god knows,
the rain tries.

Angela Arnold

STADIUM

Men have brought me here
– my lattice view –
through clear blue air,
the sun sharp,
to the stony football field
in the low stadium
with thousands seated
on the concrete benches
in forced expectation.

I am here, where the young men played,
and boys, and my sons.

Men have brought me here.

I am here. My soft knees feel sharp stones,
I hear the air.
The dull expectation declines to silence,
like before a penalty.

The man behind takes aim.

Graham Buchan

Pedal Power

I glare with disdain at the Mean Machine;
My flesh is weak, my mood is grim.
On the handlebars I wearily lean,
Resigned for a full half hour's pedalling.
I perch on the rigid seat all stiff
Whilst the upbeat music gets me going;
And I pray that the time will pass by quick
As my face progressively gets more glowing.
Then I look out at blue sky, trees dressed gold;
At birds feasting on the berry harvest;
Whilst each turn of the pedals gets me toned
As I absorb nature at its finest.
This brings the urge, a sudden spark:
Maybe there's something in this fitness lark?

Jennifer A Miller

At the 11th Tee
(for Matthew Sweeney)

He swung the driver like a hammer, smashed
the tee to smithereens and sent the golf ball
arcing in a high majestic curve towards the sea.
'Nothing to it,' striding to the second tee, he said,
pitying the others with their white shoes they wiped
grass stains from with spittle; who drove at balls
with all their might and technical perfection
but, unlike him, got nowhere near the sea.

Not the type to brag or want to get too far ahead,
he drove eleven sea-in-ones and waited, face up
in the emerald grass, Irish rainbows glowing
on his eyelids as they curtained him in sleep …

He woke up to a putter's prodding, gazed up
through disintegrating rainbows at his rivals
mouthing idiot and twit; shrugged and pulled
his cap down low and loped along the fairway,
leaving them to tap white balls around a small
black hole. 'Where's the skill in that?' he mused,
feeling better for his nap; whacking, with a cunning
slice, golf ball number twelve towards the sea.

Chris Rice

The Patron Saint of Lost Things

Saint Anthony of Padua
full of learning as he was
and overflowing with conviction
preached to the fishes
on the coast near Rimini
and, according to legend,
they and other creatures of the sea
raised their heads above the swirling waters
crowds of them
to listen to him

so eloquent he was
so logical
his sentences threaded with light
following huge gravitational pulls
quoting precedents and
making promises
speaking to them directly

the spotted wrasse
the striped wrasse
the stargazer
the common eel

the cetaceans and dwellers of the abyss
the chambered nautilus
the octopus
the Portuguese man of war
and the moon jelly

so beautiful he was,
inclusive,
grammatically sound and self-assertive
his beard flowing in the wind
his mind in flight.

Daniel Richardson

Vision (That Was Planted in My Brain)

Strange how a sound you can't hear
can take you to somewhere you're not
if you'll just let yourself go.

The haunting tune of *El Condor Pasa*
comes into my mind, and suddenly
I'm back at over 4,000 metres on the *altiplano,*
approaching a bend at a stream crossing.

Sky clear as glass, that cold cobalt blue,
and along the earth's rim the improbable *nevados*
– ice-capped volcanoes – forming a backdrop,
and the *bofedal* – how can running water be so cold?

And then, round the curve of the gravel road,
a ruckus of six huge condors,
the abrupt appearance of the Toyota,
panic, the scramble to get away from a dead *vicuña,*
the moiling rush, desperate beating
of black wings launching into soaring flight,
an effortless scatter to the four winds.

Now, aloft, eyes closed, someone who is not there
is playing the Andean pipes they do not have.
I hear every note; the unworldly music fills all space
from the far horizon, across the endless sky
to the depths of the dark stream.
The emptiness and, listen, *the sound of silence.*

Philip Dunkerley

Wind Farm

On Happy Jack Road
the great wind turbines, like apocalyptic herons,
big-beaked birds that eat everything,
even the sky, sweep across the highway.
They stand so close to the shoulder
the shadows of their hungry wings
cut our path to pieces:
swooosh! in front, the road ahead sectioned;
swooop! behind, at the bumper, the past receding,
portioned out to orphan-memories.

But we know better, don't we?
It's all oil and gas in Wyoming,
roughnecks and roustabouts,
in a state where most of a town's treasure
is in pumpjacks.
I sit behind a pickup heading out Wind River way,
or to Rawlins, and he has a sticker on the crew cab
that says, Paid for by Oil & Gas.

The wind holds its tongue until the early morning,
when it moans across sagebrush flats,
three days straight, gusting to fifty.
It has tried to tell us, shoring snow,
snorting and kicking dirt like an unbroke pony:
sometimes you can't tell the difference
between what you are
and what you think you are.

I should know, gripping the wheel of my own truck
on Happy Jack Road,
eight years a homeowner, black coffee on the terrace,
watching the sun in its tight circle.
Yes, you know better, says the Laramie wind.
This was always you,
the past peeling off behind like ropeburn skin,
the blacktop slipping under these spinning tires
like truth.

Kat Couch

THE WINDS

The four winds
fought for the air   whipped it
this way   and that

tore at the breath of each
wrenched at the stem
tortured every letter to the death
blew worlds away   and wonders

sent fates and petals flying   felled
men in the midst of life
flung towers to the ground   swept
the tears from every face

that dared to cry

ate into every stone   etched its way in
to the hidden corners
of the mind   muscled through
to the heart of things

wrested song from itself   wrung
from the poem the power of words
poured into space
ripped the dead   from death

from every bygone day   its by

from every cry   its face

every flower   its thought

from every nil   its nought

Ray Malone

The Red Door – Old Rowntree's Factory

THE TAIL END OF HEAVEN
(for Ida (Kirby) Garland 1919-2008)

And then it is like an earthquake, the floor shakes. The lads get excited, the lines waver, the concertina fades, the squire yells, "Stop! It's them bloody Whitleys taking off again."

The young lads are coming on a treat when we practise.

"John, keep the line straight before you cast out."

"Dick, your hanky goes the other way, I've told you!"

I want it to be the best, to lift the spirits of those watching, to get them tapping their feet, joining in the songs, to be roused by the whistle, fiddle, concertina, all spangling the spring air. When you jump, when you step, when you turn, the earth throbs with you. It's as if a man is flying.

The music stops. We rest on the benches in the village hall.

"Must be grand up high in them planes." I speak my thoughts aloud.

"I'll be signing up with you then, Pat." Norman's just left school.

"Farmers, they're reserved occupations." My young brother, Billy.

"Don't forget," Herbert, the squire, wags his finger in the air. "Don't forget, I've seen it before; anyone can see what's coming and where it's going."

"That high in the air, what a chance!" Norman's met with a general murmur of agreement; we all look up as if we might touch the planes, not just feel and hear them.

They say I could easily be blown away by the wind. Dad says I have the height but not the muscle. Billy, he was always solid, never had the look of a light-footed dancer but he started in the team with me. Herbert, said to dad, "I'll keep both of 'em. They must practise."

"As long as they carry on with the farm work." Dad looks over at me. I keep smiling, always the best way.

As though dancing would be a chore. The hours disappear into nothing, not like school where the days were as slow as the summer beck water coiling round a stone.

It's the same with the singing, learning verses as quick as any of them. The scythe tucked away, the evening holds the promise of a jug of beer, singing, more beer, more singing, laughing, joking.

Billy won't sing, he practises and practises the dances, both of us skip and jump in the yard, jump and skip in the flagged kitchen, mother carting the pot to the oven,

"The pair of you! Let me by."

But she scrubs the white shirts and trousers; we'll measure up to the other Morris sides, we won't be the ones whose shirt sleeves fray, whose shirts are grey.

"Pat!" At dawn Billy shakes me, more than once. Eyes half open, I know he's dressed, shaved, and means business.

"It's Whit Monday, 's the dancing." I try imploring, stretching out both arms, a Jesus on the cross. Billy yanks off the sheet and blankets, laughs. "Beasts don't wait, Pat."

Mist lies distant in the dip of the field sloping down to the river; it'll burn off later. Jeff, playing concertina will sweat; the dancers will puff and drip. I squeeze, splash into the bucket, going through the dance steps in my head, the choruses, names of figures, jiggling a foot nearly upsetting the stool. My hands tug to the beat. Billy's got through more of the beasts than me, he won't sing or dance while the work's to be done. Those men up in the sky, Billy's not one of those men, he's a farmer right through. He's not mad for it, like Norman. There'll be plenty of Normans. They'll get by without us. When Dad's had enough, me and Billy we'll be like Jack Spratt who could eat no fat and his wife who could eat no lean, we'll work this farm together.

My mucky boots off and I'm upstairs to get into kit, black dancing shoes, baldrics crossed, bell pads on the shins. Dancers jingle, converge on the Crown, a day's dancing ahead.

As I jump high Billy is landing, and for a long second I am floating, while the top four men cast out like ducklings imprinted on the leader. In the coming together we hold fast to the slick of another's arms, closer in than friends, loving the swing and twirl and thump of flesh, skipping backwards against the breeze of the man dosi-do-ing round me. Behind me a laugh; to the side a splutter, so I know someone's made a mistake. Now I've a yen for another dance but a beer thirst calls us to a stop, and I'm ready too for a sweet ham sandwich or two.

At the tables and benches in the paddock, behind the Crown, the afternoon sun is fierce, the sour sweat of a dozen men rivals the faint smell of old manure. Leaning back to rub a patch of meadowsweet flowers between my hands, my fingers bear old stains from oiling the cart axle. Meadowsweet has that sacred scent, intoxicating, akin to men's flesh.

As the beer slips down we tease Billy for his serious dancing face.

"You ... you've go' a cushy life." Billy slurs, leans forward over the table, glares at me. He swings his arm towards the airfield, pointing to the Whitleys lined up on the runway, waiting. "Tha's where you'll end up." As if on cue one of the brutes rumbles into life. We all turn to look.

I seize my tankard, down what's left. "Not me, no, there's a farm to run. And I'm the oldest."

By teatime I'm ready for Mam's slices of cold beef, a pile of new potatoes and the salad from her garden. A quick scrub in the tin bath, then I'm dressed ready for the evening's barn dance, when Dad puts his head round the door of the kitchen.

"Let's have the both of you, before you go off merrymaking."

"I've got my best clothes on now! Billy's not dressed yet, he can do it."

"You're soft, a queer kind of farmer – you sort it out with 'im …"

"It's just one night …"

I tell Billy, he'll have to do the evening milking. I smile, he shrugs, and as he walks off, I shout after him, "It won't take long!" He carries on walking.

In July, dodging the thunderstorms, we've had to dance when we could. Dad isn't happy with the wheat, battered in parts – the Long Field is like a bog. Thunder is never far away, a yellow rumbling making drama out of the dogs snapping at the cattle, pouring swill to the squealing piglets and lumbering sow, hushed words at the dinner table. When Dad tunes into the wireless news he commands silence. "That fella, Hitler, he needs bringing down a peg or two. We'll see to him."

We've been dancing with the Great Topham side today. Billy's stayed behind to help Dad with the pigs and clean the horses' tackle. I've taken one of the plough horses and the big cart to get us all over there and back. Between the storms there's not been much of a gap, we've had to stop dancing, sing along instead to the concertina and fiddle in the pub. All my money gone; borrowed more for ale.

I walk back in to Dad washing his hands at the kitchen sink. Tea's laid out ready. Mam stiff, with her back to me at the range. Billy is sitting at his usual place, his lips tight, his face in the shadow of the bright evening sun, the kitchen saturated with it. He stares down at cold bacon slices and thick slices of bread on his plate.

"Wassup?" I'm ready to eat or sleep or both.

"You might well ask!" Dad flings down the towel on the wooden drainer, turns to me. We're like cowboys facing each other in the dust, seeing who's quicker on the draw.

"It's war coming." No talk of that fella Hitler. "Some'll have to do their bit."

"We'll be working the farm."

Mam places the bowl with the hot potatoes on the table. Billy doesn't budge.

"You can't manage without me and Billy."

"Billy'll stay. That's all we need. That land's gone over for the planes, four fields gone."

"I'm the oldest." I catch the begging in my own voice.

"Is your head always in them clouds? The ministry's left us twenty-five acres of barley, a dozen milkers with tuppence-ha'penny pasture." I've never heard Dad's voice so low, so fierce. "It's what's left. Billy can do that on his own – you'd be bloody dancing …"

"They can't call me up. Farmers, they're a reserved occupation."

Only weeks later, the postmistress hands me and Billy our letters. I rip mine open straight off, sit back down to polish off the fried eggs and bread so they don't go cold. The nights are drawing in; mornings clear but cool. The wheat got a bit of battering but with the three of us we soon got it harvested. There'll be frost any day now, Dad says, the cattle must be brought in.

I wave the letter at him.

Dad swallows his piece of bacon.

"This make any difference, lad?" His eyes don't stray from his mug of tea.

"They don't want me."

"And we do? If you're not dancing, you're thinking about dancing and pouring drink down your gullet at the Crown …"

"… and I work …"

"Billy's here, grafting. Milking while you're abed."

"So?"

Dad looks straight at me: "You might well ask, 'So?' We can't run this farm now, with three men, the land we've lost to the ministry. It won't put enough food in our own mouths, then pay out for all the beasts. You spend plenty of time talking about those damned planes. There'll be a living there. There's none here."

"There's already three joined up, Norman, Pat, and Ticker." I look at Billy. "There won't be enough for a set!"

As I close the wooden gate in the pasture where the cattle are nosing the last of the grass, dark grey clouds eclipse the sky and damp, earthy leaves drench the air. I wonder if the Whitleys will fly today; they say Hurricanes are expected to arrive any day.

Down there I'd be calling the dances myself now.

Past the Belgian coast, we're heading for 'Happy Valley'– the Ruhr – tonight.

Our sixteenth mission: Will it never end – I can't decide – or will it end any minute? Chilled, clammy skin sticking to my vest. At least I'm not like Chalky – every time he came back his trousers were soaked, stinking.

I'm cornered by the gun, the half-open Perspex, my knees in my face, the layers and life jacket doubling my size, the plane's tail end, the rumbling, growling, through my skull. Christ, the suit isn't working – again. My left foot's frozen.

A luminous sky, blue, white below and a golden yellow sinking into the horizon. Soon to be black.

When the war's over I'll still remember the calls.

We're near to heaven, above the clouds. The angels are circling, waiting out there, gliding on their great white wings, singing like sirens. It's like dancing, like ballet, but no leaping, no white kit, no laughing, no jingling of bells or yeasty beer-smell, but crouching for hours, anti-freeze lacquering my face, brown leather helmet, rough blue jacket and trousers under my flying jacket, layers all trussing me tight as an Egyptian mummy.

I wait and wait. Soon, soon surely.

A searchlight flattens out against a cloud, spreading a glow, the sky velvet-black, a gaudy orchestra of sparks cavorting and whirling in front. All the colours say Celebrate! while experience says to turn, level off, just as a shell explodes beneath us. We bank, the port wing dropping away. Out of the blackness snarls a fighter. I swing the gun. The engine wavers, shakes. We're poised, to take our turn, to cast out.

Moira Garland

Not Dancing, 1959

They seem to be made of marble,
those boys at the far end of the hall,

their black lace-ups
weighted to the parquet,

swapping secret smirks,
hands clamped into fists,

damp with desire.

Watchful from the other end,
we girls lean against the piano,

whisper into each other's kiss-curl ears,
biting our lips to make pink.

Girdles rein us in,
but our bras make breasts

we hide with folded arms.

Jenny Hockey

GLANCE

I met her eyes
and in that glance
a lifeline passed

it seemed a chance
step in advance
which could not last

though now I know
it was the first
tread in our dance

and in that trance
a lifetime passed

as in a glance

Tom Vaughan

Strictly Come Dancing

While I am unconscious in hospital, Aphasia comes to my bed and rips out my entire verbal history; whole volumes of euphemisms, clauses and verbs, adverbs and adjectives, sentences and paragraphs, whole schemes of thought.

My hair and beard are unkempt after a night of restless sleep. I sit on the bed and fiddle with my dressing gown, searching for the loophole to put the belt in. I say Baudelaire's expletive: Cre nom! Cre nom! Cre nom! The lucky ones shout out the language, as if they've discovered it buried in a forest.

At 2am, I couldn't find the words for wanting pain relief so I watched the night nurse pushing the trolley past my bed. At 5am someone was talking; a door slithering shut, I look at the ceiling tiles with their directional fissured pattern. I could be a Russian clutching an English phrase book. At 6am I can hear the sound of Orphic water and earth, my mind is on fire raging to speak, to set the narrative; but a blotter cloaks my brain, a haemorrhage spilling out of my fountain pen.

The following day, I have visitors, wanting to interrogate me. I am passed over on the main issues of the day; they talk quickly, 140 words a minute in a make do lingo, completing sentences for me, my voice preserved in a language jar. The physiotherapists teach me to walk and climb stairs. I have lunch and dinner on the ward, getting used to the rhythm of the place. A nurse comes in, about my age; a watch on her breast, crisp newly starched cuffs, freshly ironed tunic. She takes blood from my bruised arm professionally and painlessly. I focus on her elegant cheekbones, still handsome.

The staff have a meeting about me. I look normal, but I speak fragmentally, like a faulty microphone. That day my transfigured self, my interpreter's self, steps out into the world.

My apartment is reached by climbing twenty stone steps to a great front door, which swings open onto an unpainted Victorian hall, smelling of newspapers and old people. The house has a distant yearning look, as it tries to evade the chokehold of undergrowth, it slants skywards as if retreating to higher ground.

As I go up the stairs, I focus on the landing window with the blue and gold roundel. I catch the familiar smell of old floor boards, coffee and dust. My flat looks like a library, with tall egg-and-dart walls overlooking an overgrown garden. In summer shafts of dappled light filter in through the half-open blinds, gold chevrons sit on the floor. In winter, the dank aching cold brings a prospect of fog into the hall, and the cellar overflowing with rainwater, carries a lavatorial smell which lingers in my nostrils.

After Alice died, all the elegant touches are gone for good; paintings by her hanging on a wall, almost by accident, the still trembling freesias thrown carelessly into a pot, wine, olives, and feta cheese on the French table, waiting for sparkling conversation with friends. She taught me to treasure these things.

All I've got now, is a red alarm of bills:

Please ring this number today ... How to access your online Banking Digital Inbox ... Insert your password, pay by barcode. Please send your postal entries to ...

I spend an afternoon finding out how to switch on my Lenovo computer; it makes a sub-sonic noise beneath next to the Bakelite phone. I see a crow trapped in my room, a frantic tintinnabulation near the window. I listen, frightened and spellbound, tracts of time pass in its acreage.

But it isn't a bird. It's the telephone ringing and ringing. I pick up the receiver slowly, defensively. The twilight is coming; a blackbird is singing in the last light, I see doors opening, welcoming visitors, a glimpse of living rooms with their books and conversations caught in a moment between daylight and dusk, the long emerald lawns, the gardens filled with lilies and roses, their seductive scents.

'Hello ...? Yes. That's me. What do you want ...? Yes ... Could you speak more slowly ... I can't understand what you're talking about? The electric bill?'

I think it is a Russian woman. I hold the phone away from my ear to escape the consonantal harshness, the rushing pace of the words. I can see the disturbed exclamation marks; commas and full stops falling from the syntax, as the image of the woman runs before the typeface, sliding by on hot metal, the words zipping like machine gun fire.

'I've been ill ... I've ...'

I judder to a halt and look out at the riotous nettles against the beautifully proportioned windows, the wild copse, riddled with pathways.

'I've got to go. Someone is at the door ...' I put the phone down quickly.

I can understand the mechanics of the unpaid bill – the wrong password, the blocking of the bank transfer. What to do about it is another matter. I can't seem to figure it out; I can't grasp what people mean. I pay a shop assistant, and then go back, to pay her again. I try to carry on as if things were normal. After all, I could walk, and listen to conversations, and sometimes haphazardly join in.

I had a seizure at a concert. I remember a disturbance in my body, starting in my back, gentle at first, and then the electrical storm broke. I stood up, gripped my chair, the quartet played on. The spasm was doing something unimaginable with my shoulder, commandeering my arm above my head. The music stopped the people were staring. I watched my selfhood depart piece by piece, the onlookers were mesmerised. The paramedics arrived and gave me a shot, and I passed out. I don't know if the seizure is coming back.

The dictionary is open at the S's. I pick up an already sharpened pencil and dart down the page: segue, seicento, seismic, seismograph, seismic shock, sanity and then, *seizure, a sudden fit, a convulsion.* I shiver and shut the book. I make an awkward note with my left hand. My writing is an otherness, and the future of words is not safe in my hands. I've lost my ability to write quickly, and to speak confidently and without hesitation. In the old days I used a fountain pen and a battered Moleskin notebook, snug in my hands; I had control of my vocabulary, walking the line between bombast and moderation, the cool flow of my pen shaping the prose. Now there is a drought of words, and the flow of comprehension is frail, breakable. I carry on writing with my grubby left hand; my right-hand sweltering, lifting the paper. My eyes feel different lately, like telescopes equipped with parabolic mirrors that collect light from a distant source. A spherical aberration dilating my pupils, as if I was on drugs.

I received a phone call from retirees, asking me to attend a dinner for a friend. They don't know what they are asking for, but they were adamant: 'Don't worry. We'll collect you!'

The guests sat down. A crisp brown turkey lay at one end of the table, and at the other expensive wine. I sat next to a woman, about my age, in a silky mandarin collar coat, the hazy colours kept alternating between green and black. She looked at her watch, and I caught a glimpse of her hands which were smeared in acrylic yellow. Like an adolescent I struggle to start the conversation. What's my name for God's sake?

There is an immense pause, my soul going through a void, like a long freight train.

'My name ... is ... Tom Blake.' I concentrate on the end of the sentence. I remember the yellow paint on her hands. I struggle to the end.

'... What's yours?'

She turned to face me and smiled:

'Kate. My name is Kate.'

I nodded. The sentence structure is clear, one independent clause.

'... An artist?'

'Yes, how do you know that?'

'I saw your hands. My wife was an artist.'

'Is she with you?'

Men who have misplaced their wives don't know how it happens. There is a silent configuration. It is a mystery. It is like a certain line of poetry, like recalling a lover's face, the line of her lips, the wisps of hair on ivory wrists, the magnetic field of her movements.

'My wife is dead.'

'Oh, I'm sorry.'

'Was it long ago?'

I could remember the shape of the friendly words; I start to feel that I can change the world by an inflexion; but in the moment caught between

Kate's eyes, I cannot visualise the complex meaning of the words. I am in a queue to say something, and the doorman of the nightclub turns me away. I feel like Ralph Waldo Emerson, when he said how he was feeling after the stroke:

'Quite well, I have lost my mental faculties, but I am perfectly well.'
'Do I know you?' I said.
She laughed. 'Yes of course you do. I took blood from you at the hospital.'
'I remember it. You were dressed, kind of old-fashioned?'
'Is that so?'
'Yes, I rather liked it.
'How did you get here tonight?'
I looked at my ex-colleagues, standing in a tight circle talking. I nodded towards them:
'They brought me.'
'Are they are taking you back?'
'I don't think so.'
'How are you getting home?'
I shrugged. 'I don't know.'
'Shall I take you home?'
'Won't your husband mind?'
'I'm not married.'

Kate slipped off her coat and made herself comfortable on the sofa. On her fragile shoulders she wore a simple black dress, the hair was tousled down her back, a final lustre of salt and pepper.

'So, what's wrong with you Tom?'
'That's like asking a disfigured man what it's like to be disfigured.'
'Enough of the self-pity!' she chided.
'I can't keep up with the conversation! I feel like a man with a stutter in a roomful of people, trying to tell them that a bomb is about to go off.'
She laughed. 'But you're talking now, you understand what's been said, don't you?'
'I suppose so; but I can't join in a debate. That's the point of conversation.'
She moved to the wall, white with A4 paper, words with their scruffy definitions written in Gel Grip.
'What are these?'
'Things that I can't say, difficult words.'
She looked carefully at the S's.
'You can get by without these words.'
She reads out loud: *'seizure, a sudden fit, a convulsion.'*
'Are you some kind of author?'
'I was a journalist, political correspondent for the Birmingham Mail. Five years from retirement.'

'Perhaps writing is all in the past. Get a hobby; art or photography.'
I didn't reply, because I thought that writing is everything. Then she said:
'How do you feel about dancing?'
I laughed out loud.
'Dancing! I can't dance, *before* the stroke. Now, my right leg won't work properly. I'll fall over!'
'Maybe. But you won't fall over if you are with me.'

A fortnight later, I'm standing at the door of the Seventh Heaven Dance Hall, listening to the loud Salsa music coming from within; watching the carefree crowds of dancers; rag-tag glitterati, brushing past me with their silky dresses, seeking a break at the bar. I've come without my stick, gripping the door handle until Kate takes hold of me. She is dressed to kill, and leads me on to the sprung laminate dance floor.

Far away from the dance hall, the journalists sift through their copy; getting the story right for their readers; knitting a reality out of words, a ring of roses, a circle of uncertainty, a sphere of influence, a round condemnation.

I hold Kate tight, and the band strikes up.

John Whitehouse

THE BELLS OF BRESCIA

That hot Sunday morning the bells woke you.
We crept into the dining room
wrapping slices of *ciambellone*
to eat in the cloisters of San Francesco.

Inside the air was cool, the congregation arriving
as you danced on colours spilling
from stained glass.
Old ladies in black smiled, remembering.

White flowers wilting.
Medieval bells chiming plaintively,
unlike those at yesterday's wedding.
You waited whilst I recorded their peal.

You said, *silly grandpa.*
When I replay the video, I hear your voice
and the weight of a thousand years of prayer
as layers of paint flake from ancient frescos.

Clint Wastling

AFTERMATH

Francesca prepares the olives
in a garlic marinade,
scented with fresh coriander.
She serves them in the blue glaze
of earthenware pots,
draws a pitcher of water
at the *fuente* where children
unspool their lives.

At the stone house bistro,
voices, laughter again,
the smell of *guisado*.
In the light of whitewashed walls,
a young couple play cards,
her loose blouse a distraction;
leaves on the sacred oak quiver
in shifting air.

The first family return,
una mesa para tres por favor.
Tomasz fingerpicks his guitar:
he remembers the dead
but his words are for the living,
the lovers and the mourners.
His song is a prayer
and he prays, he prays.

John Scarsborough

Pizza

Every Friday evening he arrived home with a four-pack and a litre of whisky. Then he'd order in a pizza. He would quarter it slowly and deliberately with one of those wheel-type cutters, stainless steel and unnecessarily sharp. 'Just four slices,' he would say. 'I'm not hungry enough for six.' We were expected to laugh but it wasn't easy, knowing what the night would bring.

It was almost twenty years before we found the strength to throw him out. When we finally did, it was in tiny pieces. But to start with, we cut him into four.

Gregory Heath

Wetin Dey – Solomon Onaolapo

WASTE

Saul hated that six months ago – it felt to him like a lifetime – his comfortable future as a doctor had been taken away from him and, stuck in the back of a workies' van heading for a linoleum factory in Kirkcaldy, he had plenty of time to reflect on the fact that life was a hard taskmaster. Beside him two workies blethered, insulting each other each other and chatting in a half-serious, half-light-hearted manner. Opposite Saul, shoulders hunched and staring at the floor sat Phil. He was a shy, music student at Edinburgh University. Phil was having a grim time of it. The workies held a grudge against students, thinking them a soft, privileged bunch who whiled away their days in a fog of drink and drugs.

Ahead of them lay the task of cleaning up the industrial waste the regular workforce would have nothing to do with. Large, red lettering along the side of the van declared its intentions –

BEAT WASTE

The men in the van needed money more than they needed job satisfaction. Sitting in the back of the van, Saul could not tell where the road was taking him; only the driver, high up in his seat, could do that. Harry might be forced to slow down at an awkward bend or he might feel free to speed up when there was no visible danger ahead. Saul was hopeless at dealing with sudden changes in speed and was forever bumping his head against the side of the van.

From the first days Saul sensed that Harry, the team leader and driver, liked him. It was a piece of luck which increased Saul's chances of getting through the weeks in one piece. He badly needed the money to keep pace with his drinking habits and to keep the landlord at bay. Saul realised that Harry doled out the worst jobs to the guys he had fallen out with. Saul glanced at Phil. He had the look of a child who might burst into tears at any moment. Harry didn't know that Saul had, until recently, been one of those posh kids who had gone to university, the difference being that Saul's university career had come to a sudden end. Saul was careful to side with the workies when it came to baiting Phil and, in order to burnish his credentials, laid it on thick that his mother was a school cleaner.

Saul's attempt to flee the nest and become his own man fell apart through his own actions. He was thrown out of medical school for a "theft." The theft was no ordinary lump of saleable merchandise but was the theft of a leg from the anatomy ward where the leg had wallowed in a huge vat of formaldehyde for many years, occasionally being pulled out into the sunlight to illustrate a particular aspect of the structure of the limb. In explanation to his professor, Saul argued that he had only a matter of days before a crucial test to become comfortable with the physical workings of the limb. Muscles, veins, arteries, bones, all had to be located and understood. He had fallen behind and required extra studying to make up the lost ground so, when backs were turned, he slipped the leg into a sports bag which he had lined with a bin liner. Surely, his initiative should be applauded, not punished. When a fellow student interrupted his dissection of the soleus muscle, at half-past nine in the evening, Saul fabricated an accident in Junction Street in which an old dearie, Jessie, stepped out in front of the number 22 bus, sending one limb scuttling across the road to come to an end at the Tam O'Shanter pub where an inebriated client fainted on the spot. The fellow student was suitably horrified and left the room without a grain of sugar.

Revision was going swimmingly. Saul was totally absorbed in a study of the bones of the foot when his door was assaulted by Professor Benjamin Fairweather. Benjamin's face was a flushed purple as spittle flew from his mouth –

"Caught red-handed, you bastard."

Saul, being immersed in his work, had overlooked the fact that human remains soaked in formaldehyde permeate every atom of the atmosphere. Maureen, his cleaning lady, seeking the source of the smell came across the foreign body inside Saul's wardrobe, alongside a pair of minging football socks. Maureen soaked the socks in bleach before reporting the stray limb. Sad to say, Maureen suffered a series of nightmares in which a badly dissected limb chased her through the never-ending mayhem of student accommodation.

Saul let his head fall back against the hard metal side of the van, the stink of stale fags and sweat sickening him. Saul imagined he was a prisoner being driven into the stark hinterland of Siberia, tasked with making good the foundations of a railway which would bring civilisation to these parts.

One of the workies, a Glaswegian, who chewed tobacco endlessly, farted, sending a nauseating stench around the confined space of the van.

"My turn," shouted his mate, who played the same game at every opportunity.

"Light it," he shouted.

He stuck his bum in the air and, when the stinking gas soared out, the Glaswegian lit the gas with his lighter. His pal caught the look on Phil's face.

"What's up with you, student boy? I bet you think your fart smells of roses."

Everybody laughed. Phil, who had taken on the work to pay for a new cello, shifted uneasily on his bench seat.

"Sit your backside down," shouted Harry. "Have you no sense of decency?"

Saul lowered his head, glad of the silence that had fallen over them. The van pulled into the village of Puddledup where the village shop sold hot drinks, hot rolls and newspapers. The guys bundled out of the rear door, glad of the chance to stretch their legs and grab a smoke. Phil waited till the shop was quiet and slipped inside where Saul was being handed a bag of goodies. Saul accepted a card back from the shopkeeper.

"That's a matriculation card," said Phil, "You're a student, like me."

Saul made sure nobody else was in the shop. Only the shopkeeper, and he was engrossed in refilling fag shelves, clicking open the system of metal doors which made a mystery of the product.

"It's none of your business."

"But you're the same as me."

"No, I'm not."

Saul escaped outside, Phil on his tail, displaying an alertness they had never seen before as if he was the gingerbread man springing from the kitchen table.

Saul had judged that Phil was too shy to carry on the accusation in public. He judged wrongly.

For ten long days Phil had been teased and criticised and throughout it all Saul had sat there, living a lie, lending his support to his enemies, hiding behind a mother who cleaned schools. Phil was willing to bet that his mother was nothing of the sort. She probably drove to an office in a big car.

"You're a liar," he shouted.

Saul sat on a low wall some twenty yards from the van.

"Look," Phil shouted, welcoming the others into the fold.

The workies stopped their conversation. They could not believe what they were watching. Quiet little Phil had turned into a raging bull. Saul felt like an undercover agent whose cover had been blown.

"He's got a matriculation card," shouted Phil.

Harry crossed the road.

"What is it you're saying? What is this matriculation?"

"It's his student identity, his student registration number."

Grabbing hold of the wall, Phil slumped down on to its surface, exhausted. Thankfully, there was no breeze to blow him long the street like an empty chip wrapper. Harry was in charge of the inquisition, a figure of much more substance. He pulled up his sleeves as if he was about to crush a coconut in his muscular hands.

"Is he telling the truth? All this time you've been lying to your mates."

Saul caught sight of his two mates, one of whom was chewing the contents of his nose while the other blew smoke rings into his ear holes.

"No, no. I'm not a student."

"What is he talking about then?"

"I have an old matriculation card. I get 15% off my purchases. I'll let you borrow it if you like."

Harry had pushed through the turnstile into a world he knew nothing about.

"A what card?"

"A matriculation card."

Saul pulled out his wallet and fetched the card into the open.

"Is it like a bank card?"

"No, it was my student identity."

"So you're not a student NOW but you were one?"

"A medical student. I was studying to be a doctor but they threw me out."

"I know what a medical school is. I'm not an idiot. What did they throw you out for?"

"I cheated."

"So, you cheated on them too. You cheated on your teachers. You cheated on your mates. Who else have you cheated on? You haven't got an ounce of decency."

Saul shrugged, the last refuge of the guilty.

"What did your dad say?"

He thought of his dad, camped by the gas fire, trying to bring life to his old bones, his pipe choking the air, a man who fought in the Falklands, and gave his life to being a postie and caring for his budgies. He was a man who, in Saul's mind, had no ambition, a man who took the easy way.

"I haven't told him."

"You what?"

"They don't know. They think I'm sitting exams."

Harry stepped closer. Saul thought he was going to give him a Glasgow Kiss.

"You've let me down. In front of the men."

Harry spat on Saul's face. He was a marked man. There was no escape.

The five of them stood on the top floor of the linoleum factory. Harry was apportioning the day's tasks. The men were quiet. Silence was unnatural in that work space where, for over a hundred years, a continuous smashing of heavy metal had battered eardrums and throttled the life out of thinking at the very moment of its conception. At Harry's feet lay a rope ladder and a hand brush. The "props" were intentional. The group knew that. They wondered who would draw the short straw. No matter how tough you thought you were Harry had a way of making you feel like a fearty cat.

No words were spoken until Harry decided it was time to speak. He nudged the rope ladder into place before his size twelve boots.

"You're on flumes," said Harry, kicking the rope ladder across the concrete floor.

The ladder writhed like a beaten snake before stopping at Saul's trainers.

The flumes were vertical shafts which ran from the height of the factory to the ground floor, a drop of some two hundred feet below. The flumes were used to dispose of waste products which, over time, stuck to and gathered along the metal surfaces. At the top of the shaft the metal sloped inwards, like an enormous old-fashioned egg timer, for a distance of three feet, narrowing to a waist of some fifteen feet in circumference, before slanting outwards to meet the walls of the flume. The rope ladder ran its length along the inward sloping surface before it hung vertically over the drop.

Saul knew why he had been given the task of cleaning the flumes. He was being punished, the power of right and wrong firmly in the hands of Harry.

Feeling like a deep-sea diver, Saul stared into the depths of the darkest, coldest water known to mankind. He lifted the rope ladder which had hooks at one end. He attached the hooks to the lip of the shaft before throwing the ladder down the shaft, the wooden steps of the ladder clanging against the metal side of the shaft.

Saul raised a leg over the lip of the shaft, the brush gripped in one hand. Initially, the ladder was pressed by his weight against the slope of the funnel. He wondered which part of the lino making process produced the brown sludge stuck to the side. The trouble began when he stepped down the ladder where it hung free of the surrounding surfaces. He was hanging above the factory floor like an out of work trapeze artist clamouring for attention on U-Tube. Saul sent wedges of waste down the tube to pile up on the concrete floor two hundred feet below. He had to stretch to reach the sides. Sweat ran into his eyes, blinding him. The ladder shivered as he stretched backwards and forwards.

Saul had no idea how long he had been there. It could have been hours, it could have been minutes. He had to escape and, just at the moment he looked upwards, the brush fell from his hand. It clanged against the sloping shelves before being catapulted against the vertical surfaces. That will be me, he thought.

Saul shot to the top of the ladder, landing on his knees on the concrete floor. He had no sooner thanked God than two pairs of hands grabbed him by the ankles. One pair of hands was unbelievably hairy and in the series of recurring nightmares the same hairy hands threw him over the lip of the flume, sending him whirling and twirling through a dark, endless space, his body smashing against the walls.

The Glaswegian and his toothless mate held him over the funnel. He was upside down, gripped by the ankles, by two men who hated him. Both men found the situation hilarious, their shoulders shaking with barely controlled amusement.

"Get out of this one, lying bastard."

Saul screamed like a bairn having his bottom smacked.

"Oh, mummy, daddy, stop."

Saul wept.

Warm piss dribbled down his face before the yellow droplets set off into space past his tortured eyes.

The contents of his pockets emptied. Just when he thought his heart would burst, he was pulled upright and thrown to the ground. Saul wanted to say he remembered the baby hung from the balcony by Michael Jackson, a baby crying its eyes out before the uncomprehending gaze of the world's media.

The contents of Saul's stomach emptied on to the floor while, around him, men continued to be amused.

"That'll teach him a lesson, Phil," said Harry. "You'll never be one of us, mate, but you're better than him. He's got no decency inside of him, a complete waste of space."

Saul crawled away from them, seeking invisibility, a quiet corner in which to curl up. He laid a hand on the side of some massive machinery and righted himself. He made his way to an exit door in the far corner. He pulled open the door and stood at the top of a series of stairs. Like a toddler, taking his first step, he descended to the bottom of the staircase.

He found his possessions. Wallet. Loose change. A half-eaten packet of mints. A pack of three. A shattered phone.

He left through a cracked wooden door which needed a lick of paint. The sun was shining in Kirkcaldy. Two teenagers, chatting about mock-exams, came towards him. Somewhere, a phone went off. Saul answered it lifting his wasted machine to his ears.

"Hello, dad. No, I'm not busy. Just walking. Oh, they're going well. Anatomy tomorrow. I'm an expert on the leg. Been working my socks off. Professor Fairweather's been very impressed by my attention to detail. You can't be a good doctor, he said, without attention to detail. He stopped the anatomy lesson to say how I was a natural with people, finding it easy to say the right thing. A bedside manner, he called it. Yes, hope so. Should be home in a week or two. Once I tidy up the loose ends. Tell mum I'm looking forward to her steak pie. Will do. Bye."

Saul found himself on the coal- stained sand, the endless ocean going on forever, repeating the same mistakes, reaching for perfection. He passed a street bin and dropped the remnants of his phone into its jaw. He watched the bus to Edinburgh rumbling along the road and fingered the coins in his pocket. Seventy pence. He would be hitching back to Edinburgh and with his funds run dry there would be no serious drinking to ease the pain. As for the rent, it looked like his exit to Kilmarnock would be sooner than he had hoped; all birds, he argued, return back from where they started but there was plenty of time to make his mark in the world.

Stewart Lowe

Thief

It started, staring down the
throat of a swallow that had
landed beside me in the garden.
On that hot day the yellow bellows
of its open mouth glowed like
fire. Though no larger than a pebble
a whole summer had
condensed to fit inside.
So, I stole its tongue. It rested
like an eyelash on my fingernail.
The swallow made no more
sound. Shook itself, flew away.
Then began a series of robberies–

the pink lump of a heron.
The blood-red spike of a crow.
The rice-coloured mollusc of
a pelican *(that was the hardest)*.
Cigarette-ash slither of pigeon tongue.

Soon, the birdsong in this town left.
A muteness settled
over the nearby forests and
city squares. I faithfully labelled
each tongue and kept them
with me always.

My obsession outlasted the
summer. In the cooling October
I was followed by silence.
Friends and family stopped calling.
Birds grew wary to see me
in the park – always tapping at
the edges of my pockets.

Stephanie Powell

She Shoots the Crows

Says it will be a deterrent to the others.
Says all the corvids are bad buggers –
but crows are the worst.
Whip-smart and adaptable,
with a memory for faces – good and bad.

She says they can solve puzzles,
make and use tools, haven't you seen
that video with the traffic signals and the nut?
Too bloody clever for their own bloody good.

She shoots the crows.

The crows
gather over the farmhouse.

The crows
communicate among themselves.

The crows
are not called a murder
for nothing.

Penny Blackburn

Parting of the Ways

No getting back on track.
A life lived cannot just have disappeared,
and with it one's own misunderstanding
of motive and desire and how we frame our life.

The loss of a map whose route was clear,
all boundaries and side roads dissolving,
to the abyss, the crevasse, the feared open road,
seeking a safety that was never really there at all.

How could I tell when I look at old photos,
that we were always fellow travellers?
Re-establishing the landscape, so little time.
You always knew the road much better than I did.

Belinda Cooke

Spring

it is enough
if you return
this year,
cup-bloomed,
rich-red,
soil-filled

then I will know
last year
has passed
since you return,
since you are here,
since resurrected
you are not ended

Gerald Kells

Resurrection, Easter 2020

Digging a potato trench, I unearth a toad.
It tumbles clod-heavy from my spade,
skin moist as rising dough, brown
as an army overcoat. Disguised.
If I look away I shall lose it.

Twice it hops to put some distance,
then clambers into the wilderness
of shadows below the hedge.
For a slow blink I saw soil made flesh,
as Adam born from clay.

Susan Wallace

Place

When the stony track to higher ground
is ensnared with nettle and bramble,
a spiral of air takes my breath away,
there is no shelter from the hot sun,
I scramble down to the hollow way.
Enclosed in a tunnel of dark green,
I find my place round the old hawthorn,
by moistened moss and tongues of fern.
Hidden between meadows, whose golden
hair ripples, I glimpse gatekeeper
butterflies sipping at clover. Over
the hill, I know there's a cottage,
with people who love me, and beyond
them, the ocean's wide horizon.

Clare Wigzell

A Place I Know

If I still had a car
I would know
the lean into the curve
the touch of brake,
acceleration point
out of the bend.

As a walker I know
the scent of honeysuckle,
the broken sign
for the old steelworks

and the clock
the workers used to sign in.
It still keeps faithful time.

Sarah L Dixon

Street Sycamore

I love that its huge presence,
its gnarled hide, stand so close to our gate.
But it's grown since we moved in.
Now a branch nearly touches a window,
roots grope for our foundations.
Already dropped flowers, wet leaves
infiltrate on our footwear.

Root and branch go on reaching further;
leafing, flowering, seeding continue.
Seedlings soon become saplings.
Unchecked, in half a human lifetime
they'd turn house and garden to woodland.
So I pull up its rabbit-eared progeny
whenever I see them. The tree can take it.

It can afford to be patient.
I'll be dead and hollow long before the sycamore.

Emmaline O'Dowd

Elder Mother

Approach her with care.
Boundaries will dissolve and reform as you enter her realm.
Lay a silver coin at the base of her trunk.
You're here to honour the December moon.
In May you packed your wounds with the sting of new growth.
On Midsummer's Eve you drank wine beneath her flowering stars.
The Elf King beckoned from the haze of the otherworld.
You very nearly followed.
By Samhain, the bones of her leaves had risen to dance on the wind.
Now her drapes' glossy beads stripped by starling and thrush.
Uncloaked, she reveals her true and wizened self.
She knows what it means to be hunted as a witch.
Touch the secret buds she keeps in reserve, their knotted gleam.
Your shadow has crossed over into hers.
Some days it's enough just to breathe.
Offer up a strand of your hair.
The half-moon clippings of your nails.
Before you take even a sliver of her bark, a pact.
Sealed with your blood and her sap.
To give back your own wood.
When you become tree.

Victoria Gatehouse

101 Harper Street

HAWTHORNS

Through winter
their spiny blackness
is capped by snow and frost
until a gentling thaw
brings tight sprigs of green,
our 'bread and cheese'
chewed on the way to school.
Close after comes
that watercolour wash of fresh leaf,
a congregation of tiny hands
whose uplifted palms
are open to the sun.
By Easter thorns are hidden
and May brings their blossom,
that overwhelming white
of mayflower.
Soon, hawthorn is forgotten,
dwarfed by beech and elm and oak
in the warmth of summer,
yet in the year's end cold
its berries gleam,
blood-jewels in the hedgerow,
before just bare black needles
waiting to fledge again
in that green flush of hope.
Palms, and thorns, and blood,
every year the same words,
the same story,
as if ordained.

Ken Gambles

THE OAK SAID

Branch out, now – leave the box, stay sane.
Open the door and walk out on your own.
Know the power of a river full of rain;
cross the river, stone by stepping stone.

You're barely a sapling, not yet fully grown;
a leap may seem to go against the grain,
but roots need room to spread: the pot's outgrown.
Branch outside the box, stay sane.

Go where you can breathe, where you'll sustain
your passion. You've miles to go and skills to hone.
They'll cut you to the ground if you remain:
open the door and walk out on your own.

New leaves will grow, so let the old be blown
away. Find your escape route; explore the lanes,
the sacred springs and lakes no one has known.
Feel the power of a river full of rain –

the power of water, of the moon to wax and wane.
Divine it, draw it in, and when you've sown
and watered seedlings across the wide terrain,
it's time to cross the river, stone by stone.

Make just one magic wish, and once you've flown
you'll see, spread out before you, our domain.
The wildwood welcomes you: you're not alone;
send out shoots and tendrils once again.

Branch out now.

Julie Venner

The Wild

A blur the moth's wing beats, and there's a joke
about opening your wallet.
A worshipper of artificial light,
does stunts and walks away from crashes.

At night bats out to get him and he steps
into the traffic like a poet away
with the fairies; when he lands it might
be from inspiration. A lunatic he struggles

to get out of the straitjacket of himself
on the sill, sitting back down with a bump like a child.
All morning he could be trying to bribe the glass
to let him out like the jailed the jailer.

In bedrooms, bathrooms, boardrooms the wild.

Geoffrey Loe

The Poet, John Barlas, Arrives at Gartnavel Asylum

East Wing has crenulated towers.
    They knuckle an unflinching sky.
Their shady echoes gnaw the grass.

He's always loved Phantasmagoria.
    Dusk; old Sun's magic lantern seeps past
high panes, charcoals him on the wall;

by day his shape is an elegant silhouette;
    by night it is a blur of death mask.
He twitches in the ribcage of his bed.

He says he tells the Ripper what to do,
    then denies it all. The doctors observe;
at supper he is God, then poet, then sedated.

Though the shine has left his skin,
    mirrors lurk in fragments of his verse.
Larks and lilies sing out of the grey.

Helen Kay

PINK POPPIES

The two nurses have just left.
He needs a rest, so we don't disturb.
I peep into the sick-room and see
his reduced body propped in pillows,
that grey face, the tubing and machines.

In your sunroom we drink coffee
and try to eat the cake I brought.
Outside the maple is too red,
the sky too blue. Before I leave
you give me poppy seedlings,

six delicate-leaved, tiny plants,
like cress in a biodegradable pot.
They should be pink blooms you say,
big-headed, self-seeding.
I'm watching them now, re-potted,

fed and watered, out of the draught
on the windowsill, their stems
inclining towards the morning sun.

Marion Ashton

Early Mornings

When it had snowed in the night
our bags became sledges.

Rather than trudge off on our rounds
carrying those heavy loads

we kept running back up
the steep paths for another go,

showing each other our breath
and pink hands.

Our muffled shouts and the hiss
of canvas on snow the only sounds,

we knew the papers were getting wet,
that they'd rip in the letterboxes.

John Lynch

Beware the Latinate

"She fled *incontinently* to her sunlit hill"
the short story began, the one I had
to read out in class. I was all of fifteen.
I started to think of a hill near home
I would go up early morning,
as the sun just reached it.

But then I got the giggles, to be told off.
Son of a gynaecologist, I thought of
the little pig unsold at market that went
"Wee! Wee!" all the way home.

I was an age when childish concepts
get crossed with adult ones.
The same age at which one never
forgets an unfair telling off.

Simon Currie

SULPHUR

The quick scratch of a live match
and I'm straight back
staring out of the patio window –
little girls all in a row.

Dad's outside, with my mother's friend's sons
(my pretend cousins)
the most relaxed I've seen him all year.
Girls get to choose, boys light the fuse.

Muted, we "ooh" and "aaah" at every spark
while they run around, mime at us, laughing.

The wrong-time, wrong-place soldier
wanted to get it over, get away, stay hidden.
Every Halloween I played him, in high hat and knee breeches,
knowing little of his pain or his sentence.
Then, Bonfire Night just meant my birthday,
the chance to start a fire
and have my father see
me

Tanya Nightingale

Red Handed

A dull Monday with nothing to do, except explore.
Mum up to her knees in laundry, spinner already
full tilt and foam burbling down the kitchen plughole.

Poking around Dad's shed I found sweet-pea canes
to poke things, so I poked some mud, wrote my name.
I poked a web and made the spider sneak into a crevice.

Dad had tins, tobacco smelling still, that rattled, hard
to open tins that burst with shrapnel, bolts and screws,
washers that wouldn't quite fit my fingers, tasted funny.

Paint brushes stiffened spiky as hedgehogs, shelf-hung
with a hole drilled in their handles, dangling from nails
hammered into shelves, paint tins with dribbled colours.

Using a crate, I could stretch on tip-toe, reach a tin.
I used a screw driver to lever off the lid, but it was glued
with old paint. Aha! The hammer on a chisel; splatter!

The contents covered me chin to toes, clumped some hair.
I wailed, trailed to the back-door leaving red footprints.
I must have looked like something out of *Carrie*.

Once she realised it wasn't blood, realised no amount
of scrubbing would get my clothes clean, she found
another use for the canes.

I've mixed feelings about sweet-peas.

Sue Spiers

Dreaming of Befana

            I'd pick you up
              lift you up
        and hold you there
                   tight
    if I still had my arms
           or my eyes.
     But in my dreams
            we soar
         side-by-side
on matching broomsticks just six feet
  over
an ocean
  not even on the map
                    yet
Greek-island blue
 deep, fathomless
        and as wide
             as we'd ever
need
          and together
           we'll never
       get tired
       of flying.

Roy Duffield

ENFRANCHISED
(For Rosie)

My daughter's polling card arrived today.
She held it like an invitation, thrilled,
As if she'd been invited to some 'do'.
Eighteen, a grown-up at last, she smiled,
Proud to be part of the electorate.
To her it seemed a cause to celebrate.

Finally, officially, an adult.
That card she held, there in her hand, was proof.
I watched her, remembering how it felt,
Such youthful optimism. I had to laugh.
She dreamed she'd shape the future with her kiss.
I knew that all she'd do was make a cross.

George Jowett

My Muse

sleeps in
comfortable under covers
and snoring artlessly.

I pretend
a noisy accident
to wake my muse

but it sleeps on.
I could tap its shoulder
but it just mumbles

not to bother right now.
It's dreaming, and will
tell me all about it when.

Michael Penny

Another Bone

Although I try to write my love for you,
the page, I fear, stays resolutely blank;
no message from my muse is getting through,
nor is it likely to, I must be frank.
Yes, writer's block has been with me a while,
and so your praises must remain un-penned;
I cannot muster words to match your style,
or find the fancy phrases I intend.
If that's the case, I shall relinquish love
and find some other theme to write about –
instead of staring at the stars above,
I'll gird my bardic loins and conquer doubt.
The sonnet form (and love) I'll leave alone,
and like a dog I'll find another bone.

Bill Fitzsimons

TRYST

my lover's doctor
has told my lover
not to make love
anymore
that making love is bad
for our health

we must hold hands, talk and text
not spend too much time together
for fear of arousal

my lover's doctor
has told my lover
not to make love
for the moment

that we must be patient
hold out for a while
think of other things perhaps

'cause my lover can't do too much at her age,
it's her heart you see, her heart just
isn't up to it, her doctor says.

still, she loves me

my lover's doctor
has told my lover
not to make love anymore
but we don't care

today we have for each other
what no man can take asunder
we do it anyway, damning the doctor
and my lover's husband

Noel King

Me (mise en abyme)

I Want That Espresso Machine

Our relationship has run its course. It's nobody's fault – we both want different things. It just isn't fair for us to stay together. In many ways, you could say that we were the perfect couple. But sometimes, that isn't enough.

The house we had once called a home is now just a storage unit, holding a collection of things from our time as a happy couple. We've both agreed to split everything fifty-fifty, half-and-half. It's the fairest way to do it.

We start with the books.

"Can I have *Infinite Jest*?" he says to me.

"You can have *Infinite Jest* if I can have *Moby Dick* and *The Catcher in the Rye*," I say to him.

"That seems fair," he says. "What about *Of Mice and Men*? I'd like to keep that if you don't mind. I've had that old copy since I was at school," he says.

"That's fine by me," I say. "But I want *Lord of the Flies*."

"Okay," he says. "Then you can have it." He looks at me for a second in that waythat he always does. "This feels kind of familiar, doesn't it?"

I know what he means by this, but I don't say anything in response. After the books, we move on to the CDs and records.

"Let me take *Business as Usual* and *Rumours*," he says to me. "You can have everything else."

"Are you sure?" I say to him.

"Yeah," he says. "I've got most of this stuff on iTunes, anyway."

"All right," I say. "If you insist." I put all of the remaining records – everything from *Good Times* to *Rubber Soul* – into a milk crate and place it on my side of the room with the rest of my stuff. The funny thing is, I once described these records as "crappy" and "old," but now, it seems as if I want them.

After the CDs and records, we move on to some of the other household items and appliances.

I get the big TV from the living room, the hoover, the dinner set, the blender, the antique cake plate, the sofa suite, the dining room table and all four chairs, the recordplayer, the Blu-ray player, and the toaster.

He gets the smaller TV from the bedroom, the bedframe, the mattress, the microwave oven, some glass cereal bowls and coffee mugs, the Xbox, the mini-fridge, the George Foreman Grill, the ironing board, and the iron.

Most of these things were gifts given to us on our wedding day. That was the happiest day of our lives. Neither one of us thought that it would come to this.

All that's left is the espresso machine. It was an expensive purchase, one that we both put a lot of money into buying. Therefore, we both have every right to stake a claim to it.

"I want the espresso machine," he says to me.

"Why do you get to have it?" I say to him. I think that's a pretty reasonable question.

"Well, for starters, I use it more than you do," he says.

"Come on," I say. "We both know that's not true."

"I don't care," he says. "I want that espresso machine." He goes into the kitchen and unplugs the espresso machine. He holds it in his arms, clutching it against his chest like it's his baby. It's times like these that I'm glad we don't have any children.

"Hang on a minute," I say to him. "You can't just take it like that. It's not fair."

"Well," he says to me, "I just did."

"No," I say. "You can't do that. There has to be another way, a fairer way." I look around the living room. "I think I've got an idea. Why don't we both go away and write up an argument as to why we each deserve the espresso machine. Then we'll present our arguments to each other, like in a courtroom," I say. "How does that sound?"

"It sounds kind of silly," he says.

"Come on," I say. "It's the fairest way to do it. Besides, it could be fun."

"Fine," he says. He goes into the kitchen and puts the espresso machine back on the counter where it belongs.

We each go into separate rooms to come up with a convincing argument. And when our respective arguments are ready to go, we start setting up the living room so that it resembles a courtroom. We move the dining room table against the wall and put a stuffed teddy bear on a chair behind it. Then we use some boxes to make two tables.

One for the defence. One for the prosecution.

I sit down behind the prosecution table while he sits behind the defence table. "Who gets to go first?" he says to me.

"You can go first if you like," I say to him. I only say this because he let me have what I wanted when it came to most of our other stuff.

"All right, then," he says.

He gets up from behind his stack of boxes and begins to pace up and down in front of the stuffed teddy bear that's acting as the judge. There's also a jury made up of all of our broken and unwanted possessions – a broken paper shredder, a lamp, an old gym bag that's seen better days, a small side table, and a dirty Moka pot.

"Ladies and gentlemen of the jury," he says. "I believe I deserve that expresso machine because I am the one who introduced my soon-to-be ex-wife to coffee."

"Objection!" I say. I've always wanted to say that.

He ignores what I said and carries on with his opening argument. "Before we met, she didn't drink coffee," he says. "She didn't even like the stuff. So I think the right thing to do here is to let me have the espresso machine, seeing as I will get the most pleasure and enjoyment out of it." Then he turns to me and says, "I rest my case." He walks back to his makeshift table and sits on the floor behind it.

It's my turn now. I get up and take my place in front of the inanimate jury. "Ladies and gentlemen of the jury," I say. "I believe that I deserve that espresso machine for one simple reason: maintenance. I'm the one who looks after that machine, who cleans it, who makes sure that it's working," I say. "He doesn't even know how to descale the machine or make sure that it's running properly. All he does is leave it in a complete and utter mess after he's used it, which isn't that often, seeing as I'm the one who always has to make the coffee. And the simple fact of the matter is, if you don't look after a machine like this, it'll break, and then neither one of us will get to have it," I say. Then I look over at him in the same way that he looked over at me. "I rest my case," I say.

But instead of going back to my seat, I approach the teddy bear judge and bend over so that it looks like it's whispering something in my ear. "What's that?" I say to the teddy bear. "You think I should have the espresso machine?"

"This isn't fair," he says to me.

"Sorry," I say. "The judge has spoken. It looks like it's mine."

He looks at me for a second. Then he gets up and heads straight for the kitchen. "Jack ..." I say.

But it's too late for me to do anything to stop him. He picks up the espresso machine and throws it on the ground, jumping up and down on it until it's in bits all over the kitchen floor. "There!" he shouts at me. "It's broken! Now no one gets to have it! Are you happy?!" He leans back against the fridge-freezer and slides down to the floor. He puts his head in his hands.

I go into the kitchen and sit down on the floor next to him. He looks up at me. "Do we really have to do this? Do we really have to do this?"

I don't say a word – I just put my arm around his shoulder and hold him for a while.

I put the kettle on. Then I open a jar of ground coffee and scoop a generous amount into the filter. When the water's finished boiling, I pour it into the tank until it sits just below the pressure release valve. I assemble the Moka pot and put it on the stove. Then I turn on the gas. I wait a couple of minutes until thick black liquid starts to ooze out of the funnel and into the top chamber. As soon as the coffee begins to spurt out of the funnel, I turn off the gas and run the tank under some cold water. I dry it off with a tea towel, and then I pour rich espresso coffee into two small cups, adding a drop of whiskey to both.

I hand him a cup and sit back down on the floor beside him. We clink our coffee cups together and sit quietly for a while. The pair of us keep on drinking until the house is all but empty. And so are we.

Thomas Morgan

IN THE STRANGER'S HAND
(to the unknown Frenchman)

Three hours we stood waiting
for the empty Paris train and when,
at last, it rolled into the dusty station
it was full to bursting,
having travelled slowly up through Spain.

Pressed close in corridor spaces
we stood once more waiting.
With the first wild lurch
I reached my hand behind
for the steadying bar.

A hand untangled mine and held it tight
against the journey's jolts.
Thumb touched thumb, fingers circled my palm,
stroked from wrist to roots,
exploring the intimate spaces beyond.

Two hands entwined, easing the weary hours,
pulling me out of the train and time.
At the final halt the hand held firm
for the one last jolt, thumb brushed palm
and my hand was once again mine.

My hands took charge, moved bags,
carried my friend and heaved us
to train, to Calais, to boat –
across the rough sea that unknown hand
touching mine steadied me.

Now this familiar hand circling my palm
revives the stranger's close touch,
the gift and the loss of that hand
sustained in a crowded Paris train.

Heather Deckner

WAITING ROOMS

No-one knew where it all came from.
Some said an extraordinary fluke of gambling,
High-end, pink diamond crime,
The chic and languid criminal everyone roots for.

Others that it went back to fourteenth century nobility.
He was cancelled at birth.
There was no mother, no father, no great aristocratic aunts
To confirm or deny,

No mention in the genealogies of the gentry.
Perhaps he was too rarified to be born at all.
Anyway and nevertheless, fabulously wealthy,
Because wealth is always fabulous,

He dipped his pocket to buy one of those mansions
That have forty-eight bedrooms.
Angelic estate agents talk only of wings.
He needed somewhere vast to be alone.

What caught his dead eye
In the golden bumph to his palatial future
Was the curious feature
Of eight *waiting rooms.*

There is only so much reception a man can take.
But waiting rooms?
Was it once home to a flock of dentists?
Will there be a tattered range

Of old *Readers Digests* and fingered *Woman*
Piled high in the corners,
With chairs marking the rim?
Will the ghosts fire up their

Sizzle-drills in the dead of night?
But no, just empty rooms,
Waiting to be given a meaning.
That must be what they meant.

Peter Datyner

Angelic Spaces and Infinite Geometries
(Title after an exhibition at Mazzoleni Art, Albemarle St, London 28/9 - 18/11 2016)

You would think Angels need large spaces
to fit into – all those wings and swords and words
from the Almighty – yet they move through
the slenderest opportunity to gain
a glimpse of how it would be
to feel like a person feels;
to know what laughter
does to ears, what tears
do to taste-buds.

That day when you thought
your door was closed,
one of them slipped through
the gap at its hinge, placed
its blade on the floor
and moved his shoulders up-and-down
in time with your sobbing.

Roger Hare

I'M FINE; THANKS FOR ASKING
(after Glyn Maxwell: How the Hell are You?)

(but most mornings there's a moment
when I feel if only I could cry
a big convulsive howl, a sob
with tears that roll and flood
that then I'd feel renewed
the freshness of an autumn morning after rain.

I want to curl up, quiet
until it's gone away, and you
might think you know what 'it' is
and maybe you'd be partly right.
Who knows? We don't talk about these things.

In any case, there's something
missing, something won't allow
catharsis, like when you want to vomit
and you might just retch
but your stomach won't heave
and your nausea remains.)

and what about you? How are you doing?

Stuart Handysides

Girl Before the Mirror I, II and III

'Girl before the Mirror I'

I smile at him, as he paints me. He smiles in return. 'I'm happy,' he says. I'm happy, too. Happy that he turns me into the colours of a summer day, makes my breasts so full and round. Pomegranates, I think of. Perfect circles ... the rest of me swirls, too; commas, waves, curves swept along, flowing in one clean brushstroke, just like the tips of his fingers on my skin.

Sunshine-yellow, mauve, cornflower-blue. Lilac. Purple.

'Pretty!' So pretty!

Or ... I curl in cat-like contentment, close my eyes, begin to drowse. And sleep, because I am full. Cat licked her lips. Cat got the cream.

I dream.

I dream of him, now. Dream of how we spent the sunny morning hours just gone. Relive them, it, once more.

I wake. We eat. I bathe, I dress, I sit before the mirror, to pucker my lipstick on, to blow him a kiss.

But, somehow, soon, I am sleeping again, in front of the glass. The frame round, like me, as I always seem to be, whatever part of me, here, and in my reflected form.

No. He does none of this. None of this is true.

Instead, he stores me up inside, carries me to his studio, then releases me in a frenzy of days. Until ... this, these.

Or so he says.

He says a lot of things, a lot of things get said. He saw me through the window of the Galeries Lafayette, buying a 'col Claudine' for my latest dress; I met him walking down the steps of the Saint-Lazare Metro. I was sixteen, seventeen, eighteen (I must be eighteen – the age of consent!). He isn't married, he is married, but doesn't love his wife. I kept him at bay for six months. We were sleeping together within a week. It's not just about the sex!

Which of these may or may not be true?

But there was a mirror, there was always a mirror. A mirror in the apartment he presented to me, the house I was installed in, the castle he gave me (yes, he gave me a chateau... or was it hers; mine, only at weekends?). A dressing-mirror, to be tilted both ways, all the better to see yourself with. This way, that way, any which way. A cheval, I called it. He called it something else.

'Psyché,' he said.

Laughing.

I didn't understand the word, I didn't understand why he laughed. So much I never understood… He told me that was something he loved about me.

'Girl before the Mirror ii'

Yellow, pearl, poppy-bright.
Black, nightshade, dowd.

'You took your pretty lover and made her into this. Her skin mouldering a rancid green, her nose hooked like a crone's. Single eye drab and lashless. A flaccid figure.'

It's how the Girl is, inside the mirror. It's what he's done to her, *here*.

First, she was a pastel-cloud, bursting from lusty flesh, pillow-soft, a brimful of joy and life, enough to make you smile, enough to make the blood course through your veins, your tongue lick your lips. There, lounging on a chair, red, black leather; here, reading; next, asleep, lost in a dream. Such a blissful dream! All swirls and whirls and circles, drawn with such certainty. First, she was all she wanted to be, you wanted her to be, you wanted, everyone wants … Love.

Then, *this*.

Girl still 'Girl' on one side of the painting, but her reflection in the glass something 'other'.

This. So that she reels back (Sorry, to the person whose toe she treads). Her breath snatches up, a knife twists in her gut.

A knife, a dagger, a 'stylet.' 'La Femme au stylet.'

It greets you when you enter the hall.

Something she stepped past quickly, seduced by the voluptuous promise ahead. Not wanting, liking this cartoon mess of rage, the gaping jaw, the spiked teeth, the blood.

But now she understands, wants the same thing – something sharp something pointed, something insidious. No, something far louder.

The kind they use in gangs, she thinks, with wide, toothed blades, the sort that digs deep into a body, and tears, wide and long. The kind she hates, when she sees pictures of bloody streets on the TV news. But now, now, she will walk out of the hall, down the stairs, out the door, turn away from the river, go … where? Where around here would sell such a thing? Where hipster cafes mingle with tech hubs and artsy chic. It's not that kind of place … a different kind of street. Then thinks 'it's okay, kitchen will do.' One of those smart designer cook-shops, then, full of French saucepans and Italian appliances. Colours as pastel as the girl was, is, until… *this*.

She'll buy the biggest she can find, carving, meat, bread, perhaps, come back with it tucked beneath her coat – they take your bag in the foyer –

wait. Wait until the crowds thin, wait till the guards are tired, or bored, looking down at their feet instead of the room. And then, and then …

What? What will she do?

Thoughts jig and jag, just like his art.

A single slash of the blade, down from as high as she can reach, down the centre of the painting.

Or… that jig/jag turning into zig/zag – cuts this way and that, following his lines.

Or, maybe, just cut it out, cut carefully around the mirror, around this other, leaving the Girl in her place, restored to her rightful glory. Something else to hide under her jacket, to carry away, and burn. Lay her like some suttee wife on a backyard pyre. She was, after all, as submissive as that, they say.

But yes, she will have to wait, and still it might not happen. The wire that lies across the floor might be alarmed. The guard may not falter in his duty. She might falter, turn back into the person who was appalled by such things, seeing the slashing of a work of art as great a crime as careless gangsters. Shame! Shame, too, because isn't some battered and broken and tortured mind always involved? So what does that say about her?

'GIRL BEFORE THE MIRROR III'

Wan, red, mottled.
Lacklustre, blemished, skewed.

Girl stands before a mirror, sits before a mirror. Takes another mirror – round, with handle – to her bed. To look at who is there.

'Tell me about the girl,' he asked her.

She tells …

But that was later, in that place, a lot of time gone.

For now, the girl stands, sits, kneels, sometimes, in front of the mirror, looking. *You* stand, sit, kneel before the mirror. But not in adoration. Anything but…

… but, looking tells you things.

The mirror tells you things, shows you who you are. It's what they do.

'Mirror' – a shiny surface that sends an image back by reflection.

'Mirror' – where every focused beam of light incising on its surface is bounced back in a single direction. That means you.

You broken into shards of skin, each bruised, or pocked or pitted. Your fingers reach for the slightest shred, your nails seeking its edge. Scratch, scrape, ferret away. There! … not 'there'. Dig deeper, burrow your nails down, till the blood runs to wash the blemish away.

You, your eyes, too wide apart, too close, too small. Such a dull colour! The brows above too thick. Pluck, pluck, pluck until there is nothing left. Gone!

Your lips, so thin, so pale. You hook your tooth over the flesh in the corner, bite, chew. Blood, again, collecting, drying to a scab, worse than before. More work to do.

Mirror/specular/wavelength/illusion/delusion.
'No, it's really me,' you say when they tell you, 'you look fine/it's adolescence/it's your age/you'll grow out of it/don't worry.' When *he* tells you the same things, too.
The mirror can't lie, after all.

Scritch, scratch, scritch, scratch. Your fingers dig deeper in your skin, again. Yes, you will tear strips of that skin down, down, until your cheeks are marked like some native tribesman – better than the blushed, flushed patches that mottle and daub. But still you find yourself wishing for more – wishing, more than anything, to be one of those creatures (a snake, a lizard) that sheds its outer covering… sloughs it away – you've seen it on those nature programmes on TV – little by little, shimmying out, until it, you are born again, fresh, pristine, a new start. Clean. Clean – something else you want to be. Something everyone wants to be – a good thing, surely. To rub and scrub and scrub some more, until your skin is raw. Yes, you have what you want… sloughed away. Yes! No… No!

Mirror, mirror on the wall, in the corner, in your hand. The fairytale queen/witch is not the only one who talks to the shiny glass. Glass … yes, glass is all it is. Or a pool you pass in the street, a window, or paned door. You look at them all, searching for you, wanting to be sure you are as you think you are. But yes, the polished glass at home is best. Glass is your best friend, your only friend, your room-mate, companion. Who else is there, when you lock yourself away? Who else, after all, would want to see you?

Mirror, mirror, light, lights all the better to see you with. To see you close, close, tight in, once, twice, a hundred times, a thousand times a day. Your life.

'Girl before a Mirror I, II, III'

Woman stands before 'Girl before a Mirror.' *Girl* has grown up, *girl* is okay, *girl* has been lucky, luckier than most, she has a good life, she has forgotten. Until… this. Just a painting, that's all it is, a painting in an exhibition she decided to visit. A mistake.

But no, she won't fetch a knife, that isn't who she is. Knives are for others. Dora Maar – the irony of that, Maar who usurped the pastel child as Picasso's lover. Her painting slashed as if Girl had some future accomplice taking her revenge.

'La Femme' with her stylet. His first wife, no cream for this cat, no pretty colours and soft curves; just squiggles and harsh lines, as she's stabbing and spiking and skewering her rival. Girl's turn, now, to feel the pain.

But, no, no knife, yet she understands the rage. Felt the rise of it, once upon a time, in her belly, felt the explosion of it as she slapped the face of the boy who laughed at her, from across the street. If he did. Perhaps. Or she thought. Another reason to lock herself away.

Another reason for them to lock her away, the second time, after the first, *in that place.*

The first – Girl does, too. Yes, Girl reaches her hand forward, wanting to touch the Other, wanting to wrap her hand around her, and pull her away, pull this charred, warped, festering image away, and put another, her rightful self, in her place.

Yes, *she* did this once, reached too hard, breaking the glass, cutting her hand, her arm, the wrist in between. They thought it meant more than it did.

They all think it means more than it does.

Beside her, they stand there, breathless at his genius, his achievement. His meanings. She hears their hushed words.

'… the duality of the nature of beauty.'

'… age …'

'… isn't she pregnant? Doesn't it show what pregnancy does to a woman's body?'

The writing on the wall says something, too. But she knows differently, she sees otherwise. She understands.

I'm not happy now, I'm not smiling. Here … or there, in this picture. My colours have gone, my curves crimped or fallen; nightmare, more than dream. No cat getting her cream. I don't understand. I never understand. He says it is something he loves about me. Why? Why does the mirror change who I am? Why does he change who I am? All I want to be is me. Whoever that may be …

Diana Powell

Exposure

The last subject left an hour ago and you're just about to lock up the studio for the night. The day's gone OK, the afternoon easier than the morning, more profitable too. But then the fashion work always is. You call it *fashion* to attract the girls – make them feel good about themselves, that they're in safe hands and on the right track with their career. But really it's mutton dressed as lamb.

It's hardly what you set out to do, but it pays the bills. You wanted to be a landscape painter, but could never master clouds at art school, and found photography a cinch. As long as you get the light right and know what you're doing in the dark room, you can't go wrong. Besides, who wants landscape paintings nowadays?

People are unsure when you tell them what you do. They get the portrait side of things – families, couples, pets – that you don't do much outdoor work, and specialise in catalogue stuff for underwear firms. But it doesn't take long for the jokes to start. "A shit or bust business, I suppose," they'll say, or "Well, I'm pleased you've got that off your chest." One mate you go round to have dinner with even does roast duck every time, just so he can ask, "So Harry, what'll you have – breast or breast?"

It's more technical than they think. Fixed tripod or hand-held, colour or black and white, light source, shutter speed, composition, close-ups, digital remastering and so on. But what really makes or breaks an image is knowing how much light the skin can take, what colours to use for clothing, background, make-up.

Especially make-up. When a shoot is booked, you send the girls your Ts & Cs with a contract to sign and return. In the covering letter you ask them not to wear make-up, but they always do. So the first half an hour is usually spent taking it off, which makes them all upset.

You understand if it's their first time, and don't mind that much since you charge by the hour. But if they've signed up for the Platinum service and you've got the make-up artist in, it's your clock that's ticking. And when it's a girl with no money from somewhere up north you wish for their sake they weren't so thick. But all they can see is their dream, to become the next Cheryl Cole or whoever.

They usually come with their mum. They love their mum and their mum loves them, and think of her as their best friend. True, the mums are supportive, protective. Anxious too. But sometimes you wonder where it's leading, shouldn't they be encouraging their daughter to get a proper job. And some can be pushy, with their own agenda, asking what to do next, how to get a break, can you have a word with this magazine or that. You're not an agent for Christ's sake.

You let the mothers in for the first five minutes of a shoot, when the girl still has all her clothes on and you're taking blanks mostly while coming out with some chat to settle her. "So where are you from then?" "What are you looking to do?" "Do you like animals?" "Tell me about your boyfriend." That kind of thing.

They'll have been a teen queen and the school hottie, you see, used to getting their own way. But once they're in the studio, they're a fish out of water, nervous as hell, still trying to do the pouts and poses they've been practising in front of the bedroom mirror all year. And what you tell them to do goes in one ear and out the other.

So the chat is critical. It helps builds up their confidence, the mums' too. You usually wear a wedding ring and slip in that your wife'll be along later or that you had a nightmare weekend as coach to your son's Under-9s side. The mums like that. A single guy would be a lone wolf. A shark. A predator.

After the initial shoot you take a break before the main one. You have a think about all sorts. Light levels mostly. Skin tones of course. Which colours would suit them. Do they have a natural smile or not. What angles would work best. Looking up or down. What do you need for setting up. It also gives them a chance to see mum alone, discuss their big day so far and hopefully agree you seem "nice" or whatever.

But then the mother has to wait with Janice on reception. No girl is going to undress and feel sexy with her mum fidgeting in the wings, and it doesn't allow you to focus either.

This is where it counts, and the girls know it. You start with the clothes on. Then blouse undone. Then just bra. Then topless. By now they're more or less used to the camera, studio and you – and feel it's ok to unbutton their top and take off their bra because you're a pro and have seen it all before.

You usually get all the shots they need in the first ten minutes or so, with the missy standing, full-on. But you spin the session out to take it into a second hour, and get her to do different poses. Looking up. Looking down. Looking over the shoulder. Looking happy. Looking sad. And all over again, with her sitting down.

"Once more," you say, "but with feeling. That's it. Hold it. Perfect."

They're up for it now, confident as hell. They believe this is acting, and have just found themselves as the new Kate Beckinsale – that today is the first day of the rest of their lives. But really, they're just sitting there doing whatever you tell them. "Crawl across the floor on your hands and knees" you could say, and they'd be off in a shot. As much brains and initiative as Dumbo the Elephant.

Once the session's over, you're straight into post-production, sifting through the images on-screen. You like to start when they're still getting changed, just in case the resolution means their skin has come out in corned beef blotches and you need to take a few more shots. But to be honest, that happens rarely nowadays. And there's not much a bit of air-brushing can't put right.

Do you fancy them? They're good-looking, most of them, sure. But they're also too young, all skin and bone, or already have Bo-tox lips and over-sized implants that are only ever going to get them a job in porn. And you lose your appetite somehow when it's handed to you on a plate. Besides, you're no spring chicken these days. And more to the point, you've got a business to run, mouths to feed, contracts to manage. Reputation is everything in this line of work.

Not that you don't have a laugh. Sometimes Janice will have a lark on the computer, sticking the heads and shoulders of the ones with bossy mothers onto different tits, under the title *A Right Pair*.

That's about it really. Janice sends on the photos a week later for them to tout to the modelling agencies, tabloids, gents' magazines, poster printing firms, whoever. She could do it sooner but you like to be 100% sure the money has gone through clearing first. You never know.

Do they find success? You've no idea. You never see them again.

Will Kemp

AFTER THE PANDEMIC
("I will arise and go now" W.B.Yeats)

When it's finally all finished,
I dream of heading North
Where the wild winds aren't diminished
Where the oceans swirl and roar

Where the white unleavened sunlight
Pierces cracks in grey flecked clouds
Where gannets soar in streamlined flight
Across the broken shroud

Where squalling gulls call daybreak
Where a seal's sad cry heralds noon
Where darkness arrives before evening
Where poetry's written in runes

Where islands layer on islands
Where bright strands layer bleach white
Where mist rolls in whispers across silver sand
Where the runes are written in light

Where the earth and air co-mingle
Where fire and water burn
Where waves crash on soft shingle
Where all once held sacred returns

I will arise and go there
I will go once again to the North
Where the wild winds aren't diminished
Where the oceans swirl and roar

Eileen Neil

ASHES TO GO
(Philadelphia, 2/16/21)

It catches my eye, awkwardly hand-lettered, mounted on
a rough plank. I nearly swerve the into the snowbank, overcorrect
the wheels and swerve a little too close for comfort toward
the people clustered with their coffee cups and cigarettes
outside the behavioral health center on the opposite
sidewalk. He stands a few yards from them, within the
wrought iron gates of a church. A large man, shouldering this
burden, face double masked, blue surgical and black cloth.
Crisp white vestments, gilt trimmed, peek out beneath a heavy
camouflage parka. A thick rosary chain hangs limp at his side.
St. Luke's ox scowls benignly from the archway behind him,
St. Luke, the artist and physician; his priest does not speak,
he beckons with his sign: *Ashes to Go*, and I am tempted
to stop, wondering at this offer, what ashes, whose? But I have
patients to see, and the icy roads already have me running
behind. And that song from another plague is ringing my ears,
ashes, ashes, we all fall down.

Kelley J White

Reviews

Also received but not reviewed this time were *The End*, by Gareth Writer-Davies, *A Square of Sunlight*, by Meg Cox, and *Mollusc* by Mark Totterdell. As noted previously we receive more review copies than we can place, and aim to achieve a balance between reviewing new voices, and established writers; and between those from local or micro-presses and those published by bigger named funded publishers. If you are interested in reviewing for Dream Catcher please contact me on the email below. We try to avoid people simply reviewing their mate's new releases, as this puts at a disadvantage those who don't have contacts in the field of literary journals; if you, or a friend, have a book you would like us to review you can send it in, and if it gets picked we will find a reviewer for it.

I can be contacted on hannahstone14@hotmail.com.

the poetry business New Poets List

It felt iniquitous to pick just one of these following pamphlets, so here are very brief notes on the winners of the poetry business' 2020 New Poets Prize, judged by Luke Kennard. They are all priced at £5 and published by The Poetry Business.

Have a nice weekend I think you're interesting, by Lucy Holt (ISBN 978 1 912196 60 9) has some nice turns of phrase and compelling insights ('the unmetaphor of edgelands', 'shared hands kissing like/two cursors blinking') in poems focusing on relationships, coming of age and contemporary culture. The every-present first person narrator is confident and mature, but can come across as a tad solipsistic.

Takeaway, by Georgie Woodhead (ISBN 978 1 912196 62 3). Woodhead's practice of using the title of poems as first lines creates an urgency which shepherds the reader into dark places. This is a powerful new voice, displayed to advantage in tautly crafted poems, which juxtapose empathy and imagination. The discourse is both embodied ('the 'body / slowly turning into an apology letter to itself'), and detached enough to provide understated critique: the 'then and now' of 'The Boxer' recalls both Simon and Garfunkle's song and Joni Mitchell's 'The Last Time I saw Richard,' but is an acute observation of how the misfit and 'left-behind' live out their lives in today's society.

Aunty Uncle Poems, by Gboyega Odubanjo, ISBN 978 1 912196 56 2, is a feast of language and ideas, a richly laden table seating aunties and uncles from 'naij' next to friends and family from East London. There is wit sharp as a scalpel in 'Diplomacy,' and brilliantly understated commentary of police brutality in 'Dalston Lane' during the 'riots' when 'we …face the noise / it is a street song kettled and screeching its own broken/yes.' Having consumed this justly confident and promising new voice, I can affirm that I 'came with a plate. Gonna leave with food.'

Ugly Bird, by Lauren Hollingsworth-Smith, ISBN 978 1 912196 58 6, is a vibrant, edgy set of poems recalling experiences of childhood, school days, growing up and family. The poet cites as sources Helen Mort, Nikita Gill and Clarissa Pinkola Estés, acknowledging a sense of sisterhood. The natural world, small boys sleeping on trains and even a toilet bowl also feature in this quirky set of insights into contemporary life.

Hannah Stone

Cloud Cuckoo Café
by Linda Marshall
Yaffle Press
ISBN 978-1-913122-19-5   pp72   £10.00

Linda Marshall is well known to those of us in or near north Leeds, having been a stalwart of the local poetry scene for many years, but the writer sometimes dubbed the Poet Laureate of Headingley may be less familiar to those outside the area. In publishing her latest collection, *Cloud Cuckoo Café*, Yaffle Press hope to change that.

The collection's title derives from the opening sequence of poems set in cafés and coffee shops, some possibly real, some seemingly fantastic, like 'The Crazy Espresso Bar', which "opens one minute before midnight / and closes one minute after." This is typical of Marshall's often-surreal take on the world and its inhabitants, reinforced when she admits: "No, I haven't heard of it either."

Such flights of fancy are a recurring theme throughout the collection, quite literally in the case of 'Material Universe', in which the poet decides to "catch a bus to Jupiter / to do my Sainsbury's shopping." In 'Cosmetic Surgery' she expresses an interest in surgically enhancing her body with fruit and vegetable prosthetics, drawing on the absurd to make a point about body image and attitudes towards it, with the implication that they can be similarly absurd.

Marshall is a master of rhyme – especially convoluted and unexpected rhyme, and the humour that can be drawn from it – on a par with John Hegley. The most audacious example is in 'Rum-ba-ba', where the poet rhymes the title with "peau de soie", "chihuahua" and "pension-ah," among many others. She is equally adept with other forms of wordplay, as in 'The New Housekeeper', which gives us the "clinking of love triangles" and a "cavalry of cutlery."

At times the combination of wordplay and surreal wit is Carroll-esque, as in 'In The Bleary Sublur', with its "schlarm clock buzzburgled" and "sloopey sublimes", or conjures up the spirit of Ivor Cutler, as in 'Idiosyncrasies' or 'Seconds', which describes time "as though / used by /

someone else." The humorous poems dominate the book, but that only increases the impact of the more reflective pieces scattered throughout.

Cloud Cuckoo Café is a wonderful collection from this gem of a poet. You will be delighted by her wit and warmth, and there is a surprise waiting for you on almost every page.

Joe Williams

Cures
by Jo Brandon
Valley Press
ISBN 978-1-912436-55-2 pp 91 £10.99

These energetic poems leap off the page, reaching out their hands from past centuries to pull their reader into joyful complicity. The opening epigrams from Nicholas Culpeper and Jane Austen prompt an expectation of many echoes from previous writers, and, indeed, the copious notes at the back of book, supplying the references, could read as a 'found' poem in their own right. But there is nothing derivative here; the language is richly innovative and assertive, with a strong sense of rhythm and much alliteration. The single breathless sentence of 'Venus and Mercury' contains tongue-twisting lines to be relished for their texture alone:

> 'if the impostume
> carbuncles, cankerous ulcers, gumboils, festered furuncles,
> pus-pursed abscesses … increase …
> the Grandgore has already taken last-lease of your bones.'

Here is a script for many actors; bit-parts for Julian of Norwich, Ursula K le Guin, the Brontës, and the widow of Sir Walter Raleigh, alongside various named friends/family members. Brandon celebrates the earthiness of the human body and its maladies and eccentricities, as well as cherishing nicely observed moments of stillness amidst the frenetic scramble to live fully in the moment. The poet gives ophthalmologist Jacques Daviel the ability to see the beauties of the natural world in an aging eye:

> 'I can appreciate cloudless sky, indigo and dark flecks of corbeau,
> Drake's neck and olive, drab and noisette, creamy whites
> Turning to piss with age, feathered with bolts of red vein.'

A quibble: these days, it is the practice, maybe even an expectation, that collections will be themed, and whilst this can be a useful device to yoke together disparate poems, it can be an unconvincing strait-jacket. Brandon's collection is presented in four lusciously named parts, but I felt that these were masquerading as discrete sections, containing appealing miscellanea, which needed no such labelling to speak to their reader.

Hannah Stone

When I Think of My Body as a Horse
by Wendy Pratt
smith|doorstop
ISBN 978-1-912196401   pp 74   £9.95

Wendy Pratt is a previous editor of *Dream Catcher* and has published four collections of poetry. She is a writer for Yorkshire Life and more recently founder and editor of Spelt Magazine.

When I Think of My Body as a Horse is her latest collection and is transformative in the literal and figurative sense as the poet comes to terms with the traumatic loss of her baby. We chart the stages of her grief and hope through IVF. Horses, hares and rabbits feature in several poems; perhaps best known is 'Nan Hardwicke Turns into a Hare': "I slipped into the hare like a nude foot."

Beautifully realised is 'The Leveret Dream' in which the poet imagines, "in each heart's pulsing middle/a leveret sleeps." Hope destroyed by death is examined chronologically in 'Sixth Birthday' though it paradoxically contains much potential love, "He kisses you into grins/we pack our ordinary life into/our ordinary car." This series of poems deals directly with absence, emptiness and at the same time the process of IVF is explored in Wendy's intimate, compelling way. "This is not a Disney fairy tale. This is 100% Grimm." And grim fantasies alluded to in the final poem of the collection, 'Self Portrait with Maritime Museum Mermaid, Hull' when in conclusion to their IVF journey, "I am thirty-nine. / My husband cries, finally, over our lost babies. / We hold hands. I am swimming away."

This emotionally affecting read finds redemption and the poet is able to draw a conclusion of hope in the collection's titular poem: "I do not blame/ myself for lost babies. I did my best. / I ride my body in a slow companionship, comforting it at the end of the day / and I say, Body you are beautiful, / you are beautiful."

This collection deserves to win more prizes. I have never been so moved by the beauty of language and the emotional journey within this sequence of poems. I thoroughly recommend this collection.

Clint Wastling

between two rivers
by Nick Allen and Myles Linley
Maytree Press
ISBN 978-1-9160381-5-8, pp 36   £10.00

This attractive little book is the result of a collaboration between poet Nick Allen and artist Myles Linley. The artwork does not just illustrate the poems. Together, text and image give a strong sense of place and mood: of loneliness and wild, flat lands where human beings have always played a minor role. The two rivers of the title are the Ouse and Humber. The 'between' refers to the area they enclose, including the estuary into which the rivers drain.

The images are prints of acrylic paintings on board, or charcoal and ink drawings on paper. They are best viewed in good light as the outlines are subtle, especially in the charcoal pictures. The acrylics are mainly of marsh or river views with stunning sunsets or sunrises. The charcoal images are of more urban scenes, especially around Hull. Not being very familiar with the area, I found the list of titles at the back helpful. I particularly liked the acrylics, 'Barge' and 'Path by the Humber' and the charcoal and ink drawings 'The Kingston, Hull' and 'Hook Pasture Lane'.

The text is laid out in varying forms, from prose poem to traditional stanzas. Allen highlights rhythmic pauses by inserting spaces or breaks within the lines, and occasionally I found this distracting. Most poems are descriptive, but not merely so. The impermanence of human achievement compared to the timelessness of nature, becomes a quietly insistent theme, whether in the urban development of Goole and Hull Docks or historical attempts to tame the marshes.

It is difficult to quote individual lines as the most memorable poems, like the title poem, or 'four suns under the bridge' and 'boat graves', build up as a whole, often in a single sentence or image.

between two rivers is an interesting book I shall be pleased to keep.

Pauline Kirk

These Mothers of Gods
by Rachel Bower
Fly on the Wall Press
ISBN 978-1-913211-55-4   pp 63 £8.99

Bower writes both academic books and poetry and we were delighted to feature two of her reviews in DC 43. This latest collection shows an accomplished author at work, able to integrate the erudite (disturbing facts about air quality in 'Smog') and the earthy: ... "Home. We are in. The neighbour sees/me pull out a breast, plus the scream with milk." ('Continue on Loop.')

Motherhood, for Bower, is both an opportunity to 'write what you know' and an exploration of various manifestations of other mothering, be it avian, animal, mythical alongside human. Bower's intellectual concerns are displayed in detailed references within poems and their epigrams to factual sources – the horrors of infant mortality in St Mary's Mother and Baby Home, ('Mother/Not Normal') and 'All the Pretty Little Horses,' after Toni Morrison's *The Black Book*, a form of slave lullaby revealing 'the bitter feelings of Negro mothers who had to watch over their white charges while neglecting their own children.' Bower identifies this piece as a 'lyric essay' and this resonates with the range of well-crafted familiar and experimental forms employed in the collection. Here we find proxy mothers, wet nurses, stepmothers, changelings, and first-hand accounts of mothers, which take us deep into the 'republic' of motherhood. (As many poet/mothers do, Bower acknowledges her debt to Liz Berry's *The Republic of Motherhood*, that place with so many citizens who arrive 'not [knowing] the anthem.')

Bower's language is direct, edited for impact without loquacity: "There is a time to kill, to slick after fish, / to dive. A time to gorge, to get, / to blubber, to fill." ('Silver Seal'.) She handles the sonnet form with verve; finds strong prose poems and makes experimental use of the orientation of the page. Here is a confident and skilled poet, who one can trust (like the 'Hive Mother') to know 'the exact co-ordinates of a poppy.' This is a collection to be read at one sitting – and re-read at leisure.

Hannah Stone

The Stranger in my Head
by **Simon Passmore**
Palindrome pp 93

Leaving aside adaptations of epics like *Beowulf* or *The Iliad*, the crossover between film and poetry is a region less explored. There are the honorable exceptions of Tony Harrison's 'video poems' which despite being brilliantly realised, you never get beyond the feeling that they are conceived as poems first and foremost, with the video made to accompany. An interesting recent addition is Robin Robertson's Man Booker Prize nominated, *The Long Take*: a 220 page "noir narrative written with the intensity and power of poetry…and unclassifiable."

Simon Passmore's *The Stranger in my Head* reads perfectly well as a screenplay or short story, some form of modern noir / ghost tale, in which Ada, the principle character is suffering the drudgery of call-centre work, while also slowly, apparently withdrawing or perhaps disappearing from her life. What is less clear is what the story itself gains from being presented as a poem. It makes little use of accepted poetic signatures – rhyme etc. The lines are clipped and arranged in stanzas, and to the extent that this has promoted economy over verbiage, this is welcomed; there is admirable linguistic control, and an ability to wield a narrative. The story bowls along and keeps your interest – I read the 93 pages in a couple of sittings and enjoyed doing so – there does come a point, when you are hooked enough that you feel the need to know the outcome, how this all resolves, and another some pages later when you think you have guessed the substantial part of that.

The black and white photography feels like an opportunity missed, as it mainly reinforces the day-to-day ordinariness of the life / world, in which the story is set without necessarily introducing a new dimension to the book.

Nick Allen

New Chapbooks from The Poetry Business

From a Borrowed Land
By Shash Trevett
smith|doorstop
ISBN 9781912196647   pp 36   £6.50

Judder Men
by Ben Bransfield
smith|doorstop
ISBN9781912196548   pp 35   £6.50

Frank
by Chrissy Banks
smith|doorstop
ISBN 9781912196838   pp 35   £6.50

The Poetry Business publishes under the smith|doorstop imprint and will be very well-known to most poets. As they point out themselves, "Our poets have won, been shortlisted for, or highly commended, in almost every major poetry prize." The three chapbooks under review all demonstrate the values of the imprint – accessible price, elegant, non-fussy packaging, everything focusing attention on what really counts – the poetry.

Shash Trevett is a Tamil poet who came to the UK as a refugee from the vicious civil war in Sri Lanka. The title of the collection, comprising original work and translations, says it all – she is in a borrowed land, and the poems reflect this in terms of her efforts to make the transition and her concern to remember what she has left. This collection is one in which "new words emerged / in the borrowed tongue of a borrowed land' ('New Words, New Clothes'). There is anger in those poems which recall the events which destroyed her world – the so-called peacekeepers from neighbouring India become the Innocent People Killing Force ('IPKF'), a tank attack on a house is vividly described and when it was over and the house demolished, "…we emerged… / so cold, so numb, so walled in / that was our tragedy" ('Stone Walls'). In 'Muthumai Kolam' she laments the lost, the disappeared of the conflict.

Yet despite her experiences, overwhelming despair is not the *leitmotif* of these poems – there is an irrepressibility of spirit and of optimism. A. Athiappan once wrote that poetry was the dominant mode in Sri Lankan Tamil literature, and that it came of age in writing on the civil war. The war certainly prompts these poems but Trevett transcends the war, to write with delicacy and grace albeit suffused with loss and sadness. In 'Blue Lotus Flowers' she writes a beautiful sequence in the style of classic Tamil poetry focusing on the nature of love and the powerlessness of the lover caught in stasis. Trevett may have "abandoned two millennia / of poetry, mythology and history" but now is emphatically looking forward: "I begin to talk again" ('New Words, New Clothes").

There is no doubt that Trevett celebrates the Tamil language here – translating several poems (and printing them in the original Tamil) and celebrating the language which is still, even in exile, "bearing the music of your beauty" ('The Sinhala Only Act 1956') – but it is a continuing celebration of who she is rather than a dead-end of nostalgia for what was lost.

In a dig at the cynical disregard of the civil war by the world, Trevett writes "things happen / and the world move on' ('Things Happen'). She, it seems, has been able to move on but has not forgotten. She is like the last mango tree in a garden once full; waiting, holding memories, knowing all has not been lost: "The last mango tree knows that its branches / hold the secrets of a lost people. / It stands guarding memories, surrounded / by abandoned and derelict life" ('The Last Mango Tree').

Stephen Spender wrote that "Great poetry is always written by somebody straining to go beyond what he can do." Ben Bransfield's glossy collection may not contain great poetry but it does bear the hallmark of someone pushing his limits to find how far he can go. The poems are eclectic in their settings – nineteenth century crimes, thirteenth century Cordoba, the Benicàssim festival – and Bransfield has a good eye for place and what can define it. The marvellous 'Blundellsands' riffs on post-Christmas housewives dragging redundant trees across Crosby beach to shore up the sea defences as Gormley's sculptured men brace against the sea. An image surreal in itself but made by the delicate detail of "…dry branches docked / by bauble thread, stray tinsel strand."

The most powerful of the poems, however, cover a different kind of place – that of memory and, in particular, family memory where Dransfield seems to be mining his past, sometimes suspiciously, for meaning. Again, place is firmly fixed – in 'Nan and Granddad's' through culinary recall: "Corned beef, Silverskin onion juice / sluiced from the jar onto mash." In 'Elizabeth Crescent' the vision of a past Christmas is sharply stabbed into relief by the shrewd details, "a teak veneer sideboard", "three kittens on a powder blue collector's plate / behind the front fenders of a toy Rolls-Royce / with sidemount spare…" There is an almost sacred aspect to Bransfield's recall of detail – the sideboard shoulders "grails and reliquaries" while, mounted in corners are the "Cherubim" of "…those hanging amber scotches / a mirage of optics full and twinkling / above bottles of Dry and Babycham…"

This is not mere description for the sake of it, nor nostalgia – from the detail can be drawn whatever significance might be given up, whatever insight might be got. Granddad builds a Go-Kart and the downhill rush becomes a kind of life lesson, "to go faster we had to share, to bolt together … pull both strings taut lean back as one and steer." ('Go-Kart'). It's not always easy, the past does not always speak clearly. The goldfish in his grandparent's pond are "dumb oracles who rose to tell / but took down their pills and forgot again". ('Nan and Granddad's'). This sense of having to work hard to understand the messages given, the change undergone, in growing up is cleverly worked up. In the end though, as the Mosque turned Cathedral in 1236 Cordoba notes, maybe in the end "I am no different to before" ('To King Ferdinand III of Castile, upon entering the Mezquita of Cordoba, 1236'). Bransfield captures well the possible evanescence of it all, like bringing home the Christingles "as wax wept its way down our still burning candles" ('Elizabeth Crescent').

Chrissy Banks is similarly reflective in *Frank*; whose title carries several different possibilities though the book begins with a definition focusing on telling the truth even when this is awkward or uncomfortable. The opening, eponymous poem recalls university days and the outspoken, uncompromising Frank. Banks feels she "could have learned a lot from Frank" ('Frank'). This collection suggests that she did – Banks is unfailingly honest in these poems. In 'The Nearly Times' she recounts all the close encounters with possible disaster and death she has experienced, "How many lives is that? How many chances? /How many years was I handed to learn / how to live every day, to give thanks". Banks is a psychodynamic counsellor and trainer and there is a therapeutic positivity and buoyancy suffusing these poems – it is, maybe, a question of counsellor counsel thyself.

Whatever, it makes for engaging poetry whether covering Hayley Mills, Body Jam sessions or some event in school that caused shame. "For so long I'd buried so much", she writes ('What's the Matter Christine Fox?'). and in a sense this book is a gentle exhumation. Again, there is a focus on the past life lived but, again, not nostalgic as much as a seeking for insight. It is almost as if Banks' older self – the poet – is looking to give advice from her experience to her younger selves, to reassure that, in the end, we came through, all was well. It may have been madness to go to Clare Island but they did it, and it was "Lovely, we said, we had a fine day" ('Day Trip').

This may sound a little Panglossian, but Banks' experience of life leaves her realistic rather than cynical. "At the Juliet House, Verona" is a clever poem which explores false hopes and the infinite human capacity to fool itself if it seems convenient to do so. Though it may be that the famous balcony is a fake and Juliet is not an historical person there is always hope as "… if you write to her / at this address, Juliet will answer". Such an arch ending is perfectly achieved. The closing poem, 'The Waves,' is a sensitive study of the pressures of contemporary working in a resource-stretched therapeutic context. The sense of drowning in a never-ending sea of expectations may incline one to pack it all in but the protagonist is rescued by an image of a bus driver stopping the bus to help "a blind man in a swirling sea of traffic". A beautifully wrought poem which reveals Banks' craft and her humanity – both of which infuse this collection and will uplift the reader.

Patrick Lodge

INDEX OF AUTHORS

Angela Arnold 25
Belinda Cooke 58
Bill Fitzsimons 78
Chris Rice 28
Clare Wigzell 61
Clint Wastling 46, 101
Daniel Richardson 29
Daniel Skyle 6
Diana Powell 88
Eileen Neil 96
Emmaline O'Dowd 63
Geoffrey Loe 68
George Jowett 76
Gerald Kells 59
Graham Buchan 26
Greg McGee 1
Gregory Heath 48
Hannah Stone 3, 100, 102
Heather Deckner 84
Helen Kay 69
Hélène Demetriades 14
Jennifer A Miller 27
Jenny Hockey 39
Joe Williams 99
John Lynch 71
John Scarsborough 47
John Whitehouse 41
Julie Venner 67
Kat Couch 31
Kelley J White 97
Ken Gambles 66

Maggie Davison 5
Mandy Haggith 4
Marion Ashton 70
Michael Church 12
Michael Penny 77
Moira Garland 34
Nick Allen 15, 103
Nocl King 79
Patrick Lodge 104
Pauline Kirk 102
Penny Blackburn 57
Peter Datyner 85
Philip Dunkerley 30
PJ Quinn 19
Ray Malone 32
Robert Lima 13
Roger Hare 86
Roy Duffield 75
Sarah L Dixon 62
Simon Currie 72
Stephanie Powell 56
Stewart Lowe 50
Stuart Handysides 87
Sue Spiers 74
Susan Wallace 60
Tanya Nightingale 73
Thomas Morgan 81
Tom Vaughan 40
Victoria Gatehouse 64
Will Kemp 93
Yvonne Hendrie 18

Other anthologies and collections available from Stairwell Books

When We Wake We Think We're Whalers from Eden	Bob Beagrie
Awakening	Richard Harries
Geography Is Irrelevant	Ed. Rose Drew and Amina Alyal, Raef Boylan
Belong	Ed. Verity Glendenning and Stephanie Venn, Amy E Creighton
Starspin	Grahaeme Barrasford Young
Out of the Dreaming Dark	F.Mary Callan and Joy Simpson
A Stray Dog, Following	Greg Quiery
Blue Saxophone	Rosemary Palmeira
Steel Tipped Snowflakes 1	Izzy Rhiannon Jones, Becca Miles, Laura Voivodeship
Where the Hares Are	John Gilham
The Glass King	Gary Allen
The River Was a God	David Lee Morgan
A Thing of Beauty Is a Joy Forever	Don Walls
Gooseberries	Val Horner
Poetry for the Newly Single 40 Something	Maria Stephenson
Northern Lights	Harry Gallagher
Nothing Is Meant to be Broken	Mark Connors
Heading for the Hills	Gillian Byrom-Smith
More Exhibitionism	Ed. Glen Taylor
Rhinoceros	Daniel Richardson
The Beggars of York	Don Walls
Lodestone	Hannah Stone
Unsettled Accounts	Tony Lucas
Learning to Breathe	John Gilham
The Problem with Beauty	Tanya Nightingale
Throwing Mother in the Skip	William Thirsk-Gaskill
New Crops from Old Fields	Ed. Oz Hardwick
The Ordinariness of Parrots	Amina Alyal
Homeless	Ed. Ross Raisin
49	Paul Lingaard
Sometimes I Fly	Tim Goldthorpe
Somewhere Else	Don Walls
Still Life with Wine and Cheese	Ed. Rose Drew and Alan Gillott
Skydive	Andrew Brown
Taking the Long Way Home	Steve Nash
York in Poetry Artwork and Photographs	Ed. John Coopey and Sally Guthrie

For further information please contact rose@stairwellbooks.com

www.stairwellbooks.co.uk
@stairwellbooks